A Memoir

by Paula Pederson

What People Say

"Paula Pederson's discoveries about her father Hans have filled an important gap in regional architectural history knowledge by revealing her father's many accomplishments in the Pacific Northwest. The publication provides a partial list of a remarkable range and variety of buildings and infrastructure projects that he undertook during a long and successful career—commerce and institutions, hotels, theaters, apartments, schools, bridges and piers. Many of them are still standing, and that reflects on the knowledge and management skills of this prolific contractor.?

LARRY KREISMAN,
Program Director, Historic Seattle

"...like a long, newsy letter from a friend...precisely what makes this book so charming and exceptional, and such an addictive read."

"Paula Pederson recounts her exhaustive search for the father she never knew in a winding, evocative first-person narrative told "in the moment" as her journey unfolds before the reader with the turn of each page. Dismissed by her mother as "a struggling young architect" who was killed in a car accident and "left us penniless in the middle of the Great Depression," Domka Huculak kept the identity of the man who fathered her daughter a secret for 60 years until, at the age of 92, she finally disclosed the truth. This incredible, emotional revelation catapulted Paula into the past on an incredible quest that not only would change her life, but change how she would come to see herself.

He was Hans Pederson, one of the leading architects, contractors and builders in the American Northwest, whose far-reaching vision left a distinctive imprint on his adopted Seattle. Pederson helped define the personality of what has become the 18th largest city in the United States today.

But it is the author who we get to know best in a story that begins in Shanghai and ends in Maine. And it is the manner in which Paula tells her story that makes this book read like a long, newsy letter from a friend rather than a biography or more to the point, her autobiography. And this is precisely what makes this book so charming, and exceptional, and such an addictive read."

LAURIE BOGART MORROW, author
The Hardscrabble Chronicles

"A fascinating glimpse behind the skyline of Seattle."

HUMAYUN MIRZA, author
From Plassey to Pakistan: the Family History of
Iskander Mirza, the First President of Pakistan 2014

"Paula has a most interesting and engaging book. I

very much like the way she has combined the general interest in Hans as prominent Seattle builder with the intense personal meaning that he has for her. Paula's depictions of her mother and others is nuanced and complex; she allows the reader, who grows indignant toward their behavior, to also understand and sympathize with them. Finally, the larger story of immigrants reads familiar with so many of us: in my own case, Swedes to Nebraska and then California, Germans to Nebraska and then Spokane. For my wife: Irish to Wisconsin, then Montana. There is no end to these particular stories, and now I can add Ukrainians to Alberta and Danes to Washington.

CRAIG DIETRICH, author
People's China: A Brief History

The Mysterious Builder of Seattle Landmarks

Searching for My Father

by Paula Pederson

ISBN 978-1-943478-01-9 (pbk) paperback

SAN 990-3933

Second Edition 2017

Manufactured in the United States of America

To my family

To those who came before me

and those who will survive me.

Everything in this story is true, to the best of my knowledge.
Some names have been changed to respect individual privacy.

The two most important days in your life
are the day you are born
and the day you find out why.

Mark Twain

Table of Contents

Foreword

Seattle Poised for Population and Economic Growth

Hans Pederson reached Seattle in 1886 at a time when the city was poised for rapid population and economic growth. For much of the remaining 47 years of his life, Seattle provided the perfect backdrop for a successful career in construction, one of the best places in the world he could have lived. Hans arrived just 35 years after the Denny Party founded Seattle in 1851. The city was still largely a frontier town. Seattle's economy was then based on timber, fishing, wholesale trade, shipbuilding and shipping. Expansion of the Northern Pacific Railway to its terminus in Tacoma, 40 miles south of Seattle, was completed in 1883. Shortly thereafter, Seattle managed to force a connection to the railroad, triggering a rapid population influx in the late 1880s. In the first half of 1889, it was estimated Seattle was gaining 1,000 new residents per month. In March of 1889 there were 500 buildings under construction, most built of wood. Growth came to an abrupt halt with the Great Seattle Fire of June 6, 1889. The fire destroyed 116 acres in the heart of Seattle. The city rebuilt from the ashes with amazing speed. The fire created the opportunity for extensive municipal improvements, including widened and regraded streets, a professional fire department, reconstructed wharves and municipal water works. New construction in the burned district was required to be of brick or steel. The population in 1890 was 42,837, making Seattle the 70th largest city in the country. This almost doubled to 80,671 by 1900, boosting Seattle to 48th largest city. Growth was propelled by rapid immigration driven by the Klondike gold rush. Many city neighborhoods got their start during this period. Streetcars began providing transportation once the close-in areas were settled and growth moved to the outlying neighborhoods. All of this development was the perfect setting for Hans to thrive.

At the beginning of the 20th Century, Seattle City Engineer RH Thompson championed the plan to level the steep hills that rose to both the south and north of downtown. A seawall was built to contain the dirt sluiced form the Denny Regrade, creating the current waterfront. In the wake of the gold rush and with a rapidly growing population, Seattle was primed for a construction boom. Hans Pederson caught this wave and built a successful career until the onset of the Great Depression brought construction to a virtual halt. The rapid growth of the city's population makes clear how wise Hans was to leave Minnesota and come to Seattle.

Between 1900 and 1910, Seattle's population almost tripled to 237,194, boosting Seattle to the country's 21st largest city. Demand for new housing was enormous, creating the opportunity that Hans exploited for the rest of his life to build and immediately lease new apartments. The city experienced a shipbuilding boom which peaked during World War I but crashed at war's end. By 1920, population was up to 315,312, now 20th largest in the U.S. It kept growing until 1930, but at a decelerating rate. After onset of the Great Depression, growth virtually stopped. The Depression sets the stage for Paula's mother's choices.

Robert Wiley III

PART I

LIVES GONE 1998-2008

1. Goodbye Mother

He left us penniless in Seattle in the middle of the Depression. That's what I thought.

When I was a little girl, Mother told me that my *real* father, Hans Pederson, had been a struggling young architect who was run down by a car before I even took my first steps. I knew she was lying because of the mask that crossed her lovely face whenever the subject came up. Mentioning my father seemed to cause her pain, so I stopped asking. Since I was the child of a man who had caused my mother such anguish, I vowed I would not add to her misery. I buried my curiosity in the depths of my child mind, feeling shame for the need to know.

The truth about the true identity of my father surfaced in bits throughout my life, but the essential mystery remained for another 60 years.

Mother married Everett, my stepfather, in Singapore when I was two. My half-sister, Cookie, as she's always called herself, was born in Honolulu two years later. We had an interesting and comfortable life and I grew to adore my stepfather. In 1998, when she was 90, Mother asked me to spend a month in her Greensboro, North Carolina apartment during the wedding of Cookie's daughter, Jody. My poor mom's health was failing, so I was pleased that I could come and help her spend a few more weeks in her home of 37 years.

I had no idea that this time with mother would reveal secrets that would catapult me into the search for my father Hans Pederson. I learned nine years later that my father, known as simply Hans to most everyone, was one of Seattle's foremost builders in the first half of the 20th century. One of the 40+ buildings he worked on was the six-story King County Courthouse in 1930. After that, no other contractor built another major building in downtown Seattle for the next 20 years.

———

Her face etched with struggle, Mother rests on her pink velvet couch as I place her Chinese cloisonné bowl on her lap. Covered with painted peonies, lined in blue, it holds the medications Cookie has sent – Imodium, Premarin, Furosemide, Lasix, Rhythmol, and Prozac. Mom's hand shakes. She drops a pill into the center of a rose on her floral rug. I pick it up and offer it on my outstretched palm.

"No. I'll take it when I'm ready."

"Please, Mother. Please keep trying."

One by one, her friends have moved to life care. "I don't want to go to one of those places. I'm afraid I'll just give up," she's always said. But it's too late for life care, so we're moving to Plan B. She'll live with my sister Cookie.

She runs her gnarled hand over a needlepoint cushion. "Come live with me here. Don't make me go to Cookie's." The oxygen tank wheezes. A giant spider on wheels, its 30-foot cord allows Mother a modicum of freedom to move. She's tethered to the hulk because pulmonary fibrosis is robbing her of the ability to breathe. In and out, in and out, it wheezes.

"Mother, we talked about you moving back to Maine with me, but you said no. Too cold." Guilt washes over me. Actually, we didn't talk that seriously about her moving to Maine. I have a job, and my condo is not set up for an invalid. Cookie has a downstairs room and bath for Mom. I talk myself into thinking this is the practical solution. Little did I know.

My mom sets the cloisonné bowl on the table. "Remember," she says, "I've labeled all my things with one of your names." Scanning the living room, she takes inventory. Most prominent is the massive gilt-framed snow scene above her velvet couch. It is a peaceful painting of a woman walking down a snowy road in light and shadow in Lillehammer, Norway, painted by the Danish artist Peder Mork Monsted who lived from 1859-1941. A landscape oil painter, he is famous for the clarity of light general to the painters of this "golden age" of Danish painting. I read that his paintings of beautiful naturalistic scenery made him the leading Danish landscapist of his day. He had a remarkable eye for detail and color.

She scans the room and takes in the rosewood ancestor chairs beside her satin drapes, then the curio cabinet filled with ivory and jade -- the door still scarred by the jagged crack across its glass that she's never repaired. All those trophies she collected during her years in the Orient with the man I know as Dad. Even though I'm technically Everett's step-daughter, he never made me feel less than cherished. I wonder if he felt the same curiosity about my mother's previous life with my biological father

Hans. Whatever Everett felt, he treated me as his own and I never doubted his love. We had a special bond. I miss having that with mother. I ponder why, but never quite understand how a mother can remain emotionally estranged from her own child. I never got the feeling that Everett resented my curiosity about my father. Everett knew he had my heart.

1939 Manila: Everett (40) Paula (5) Doris (31) Cookie (1) passport photo

To Mother's dismay, Cookie and I insist she must vacate her apartment before we divide her beloved possessions. I dread this task. Mother's been switching her labels around for years. My concern is less for her treasures than for our family cottage in Maine. Mother and Dad signed it over to Cookie and me twenty years ago before Dad died. Sharing the place has never worked. Different families. Different lifestyles.

The click of a key in the lock announces another visit from Cookie. She dumps her purse on the hall table and heads for Mother. "You forgot your Rhythmol again." The pill still sits in the cloisonné. She turns to me and whispers, "You've got to watch her," and walks the few steps to the kitchen to avoid a confrontation in front of Mother.

I follow and lean against the sink. "She wants to decide when to take it herself. Why so many pills, Cookie? Why estrogen? Why Prozac? She's under hospice care. Why dope her when she's feeling good?"

"It's my job to keep her alive." My sister pushes her hands out to fill the doorway. She's tiny, but feisty.

"Does she have any choice?"

Cookie backs off and points to the stain on the dining room rug. "You'd better send that out when she comes to me." I stare at the stain thinking it signifies more in this moment. I shake the feeling off and grab the coffee pot, pour two mugs, and shove one at Cookie. "Speaking of rugs, I had the cottage one cleaned. But the spot's still there."

"I've got enough on my mind right now without that place."

"I know. But I do all the work." Crap. I know exactly what she'll say next. I should know better by now.

"You ought to. You use it more." Her voice breaks. Bending over the sink, she pours her untouched coffee down the drain and shoves the faucet handle until it grinds.

I'm pushing too hard. I shouldn't mention the place the minute she walks in. We both love it. We both want it. But right now I'm here and we need to resolve it face to face.

Bringing it up on the phone never works.

Behind us, Mother coughs. She's caught the vibe. She clings to the back of a chair with one hand, then turns to Cookie. "Where's the list of buildings Hans Pederson left me?"

The list of buildings? Stunned, I press my chest with both hands. What on earth? Nobody has mentioned my real father for years. He died in 1933. Ruined by the Depression. It is now 1998.

Mother tries to straighten her spine. "Where's the list of those buildings?"

Yes, she really did say the list of buildings. I chew my lip and watch Cookie.

Cookie checks her Timex, assuming the same impassive expression Mother wears at any mention of my real father. "I should go. The florist is coming about the bouquets for Jody and the bridesmaids."

I wait, breathless. Mother has asked her twice. I try to mask my surprise and eagerness in case it startles mother into silence.

"Keep me posted on the flowers." Mother's thin voice rises.

No! Please ask again. Make her show us the list. Then sense takes hold as I realize that Cookie has control over a list of my father's buildings. How dare they? I feel the sting. My mind races to find reasons. One thought repeats. They are keeping something from me.

"The florist is probably there already." Cookie leads Mother to her Victorian chair with the carved roses. "Take it easy now."

"Check her oxygen level," Cookie mutters to the floor, hoisting her hobo bag to her shoulder as she zips out the front door.

Mother is gasping. She sits quietly until her breathing settles, then pushes herself out of the chair and reaches for her walker. "I think I'll lie down." She turns and shuffles along the edge of the Persian rug toward her bedroom, holding her walker six inches off the floor. I follow, wheeling the oxygen hulk. No sense reminding her she's supposed to set the walker down

24

between steps to help her balance. She'll just say, "I can still stand on my own two feet." Good for her. I admire that spunk.

I'm still processing why she didn't say anything when Cookie deliberately changed the subject. It's not like Mom to let anyone else seize control like that. She's either exhausted, or avoiding this newly dropped bombshell. Perhaps she has already forgotten about it. That thought is disturbing. It will be even harder to learn more from her about the missing link in my life. I remove her shoes. Mom bends into bed and turns to the wall, effectively shutting off further conversation. I don't have the heart to push her. I'll try later. I watch quietly as she breathes in and out, shrinking with each wheeze. My heart cries out, "Mom why can't you tell me about him? Are you hiding something?" I turn and walk out of the room under a confused mixture of hurt and anger.

Mother shares things with Cookie. It's been that way for a long time now, but I never suspected they'd conceal news about my father. It stings that Mom has confided in Cookie and divulged details about my father that I don't even know. When Cookie moved Mom to her house, before I arrived, Cookie tried to keep Mom there by telling me the oxygen tank couldn't be moved. Cookie and Mother are generals. They thrive on control. Me, I aim for subtlety and passive resistance.

From Mom's carved teak bureau, I watch Cookie's son and daughter smile at me from their photos on either side of the mirror she looks into every day. My family snapshots gather dust in the guest room. It shouldn't matter, but it does. I notice these little slights, but I keep silent. Head down, I think, "I need to figure out this business about my father's buildings before it's too late." Mother is getting weaker by the day.

Two hours later, after her nap, I drive Mom to her doctor, trying to think of a way to bring up the buildings. She regards the rolling hills beyond the interstate highway and says, "It's May, isn't it? Everything is still so green." She's smiling. I'm relieved.

"Yes. Tell me your favorite places and we'll take some drives." The air is thick with humidity. I had forgotten how quickly the dazzle of a southern spring gives way to the sodden weight of summer. Thirty-seven years ago in a corporate transfer, my husband Chip and I led the way to Greensboro, the third largest city in North Carolina. My parents followed, then Cookie. When we were sent north again, the rest of them stayed. Mother has never forgiven me for leaving. Nothing I can do about that, but I guess it means she cares. Am I the one who pulled away? I couldn't make my husband refuse a job transfer that meant a promotion. Sometimes such changes in our paths affect relationships for life.

Right now, this father business is all I can think about, but I caution myself to wait for the right moment. What matters now is her doctor's visit. I circle the parking lot. Mother pulls the handicapped sign with the blue wheelchair from her purse and hangs it on the rear-view mirror. She points to the entrance. "Park right there." I obey. Some things never change.

I support her arm as she weaves through the hall, her portable oxygen tank in a sling over her shoulder. She refuses to use her walker in public. Mustering all of her strength to stand tall, she tries her best to glide rather than trudge. She's still a beauty at 90.

The nurse ushers us into a treatment room. "What a pretty blouse," she murmurs to Mother. The doctor arrives.

"This is my daughter from Maine. She's come for the wedding." My mom sits straight up in her chair. She makes fists in her lap.

"Hello." The doctor nods in my direction, passes her stethoscope around Mother's back, then lingers as she places it on Mom's chest. Rolling her chair back to her desk, she fingers the side of her stethoscope. "You're doing fine. Do you have any questions?" She seems to know what's coming.

"Pretty soon I'll stop the pills and the oxygen."

The doctor tears a prescription off the pad and hands it to me. "Then you won't die. You'll just feel sick. So you might as well take your medicine and feel as good as you can." The Doctor's eyes pause on mine to make sure I understand.

Mother returns to life on the way back to the car. "Next week I'll go to the hairdresser."

"Good. Your hairdresser always does such a nice job." A color rinse will raise her spirits. It doesn't bother me, but my gray hair offends her. She thinks it makes me look old. Actually I think it makes her feel old.

The next morning Mom crawls into bed after her shower. "I want to see all the kids at the wedding. I'll give them my furniture and my curios. After that, I'll just stop taking this oxygen."

"Mom, can I ask you something?"

Dismissing me, she throws her arm across her eyes. I don't push. More and more my mother draws into herself as she prepares to leave. Just being here is all I can do to help. Again, I remain silent.

An hour-long nap revives her, and she decides to go outside. We cross the living room to the sliding patio door. I open it, and watch her sink slowly, carefully into her chaise. She lifts her face to the sun and a small smile grows.

"Would you like a blanket?" Mom is so tiny and frail it seems she might evaporate. Still, she seems relaxed, so I dive in. "Mother, sometimes I get curious about my real father. How did you meet?"

The usual mask crosses her face at the mention of his name. I hold my breath. "Oh, let's see. I think I knew someone else in the same building. I think maybe we met in the elevator." She frowns and drops her eyes. She never meets my gaze.

Gently I try another tack. "I was a small baby when he died?"

"Yes. He drove out one morning. You know how the sun gets in your eyes? Well, it blinded him, and he had an accident."

The telltale lilt in her voice tells me she is lying. A confusion seems to come over her. She points to the vine that snakes across the wrought-iron railing. "Look how it's grown. I need a trellis to train it up the wall." Cardinals flash through the tulip tree. "I've lived here a long time. I'll miss it when I go."

I remind myself that I am here to care for her — to ease the discomfort of her life. Cookie and I have no right to pollute what's left of it with our own agendas. So, I curb my desire to press her for information.

Still, Cookie has no right to keep me away. When I got off the plane her daughter Jody was waiting at the bottom of the down escalator near the baggage carousel. Her first words to me were, "It's a good thing you've come. Mom is at the doctor's with eye trouble. She's seeing spots and light flashes." Jody quickly picked up my suitcase, wheeled it out to her car, and tossed it into the back seat.

"Just what you need right now," I sympathized as she got behind the wheel.

"Well, you're here now to take care of Grandma. Actually the wedding is well in hand. We've found an awesome blue grass band."

"Your mother mentioned that you might have a pair of strolling minstrels. Violins?"

"Dad suggested that last winter, but Kevin and I opted for the blue grass."

Jody slowed as she rounded the corner and pulled up in front of Cookie's house, sandwiched between a low hill and a ravine. She raced my suitcase up the path to the front door. Mercurial as ever, she turned and dashed back to the car to head straight for Cookie's ophthalmologist.

I walk up the path and see Mother in the doorway, weaving on her spindly legs. "I'll just get my purse and then we'll go."

Beside her, my brother-in-law Dennis, assumes his usual role as guardian, standing ready to catch her if she topples. Dennis the tank. Mr. five by five. He pivots to let Mom by to get her purse.

"What's the rush Doris? He jiggles Mother's car keys as if they are stuck to his fingers then shakes them loose on the hall table.

"Why hello, Dennis," I chirp, and scoop the keys up with a flourish that lets him know that Mother's car still belongs to her."Hey, great minds think alike," I say. I wave my arm out and back, having noticed that each of us is clad in the same ocean-blue polo shirt sporting an L.L. Bean logo, mine in a small and his in XXL. Dennis is forever stopping by L.L. Bean on his trips to the market in Maine. A skilled and imaginative chef, he grills swordfish to perfection — not that I eat with them anymore. In years past

I used to drive Mother and Dad on their annual treks from Greensboro to Maine, but now Dennis and Cookie bring her. I used to stay with her while they drove to Tanglewood for the Boston Symphony concerts, but now they've stopped going and don't even want me in the cottage when they are there with her.

Dennis grunts, turns on the heels of his rubber-soled shoes, and heads for the stairs. "Come back anytime, Doris," he says. His insincerity is palpable. Never mind, I feel the same about him.

Mom hands me the portable oxygen tank. "Here, you hold it." I sense her satisfaction as she navigates the downward slope to the car, setting her walker down firmly every other step. She bends her head to step from the sidewalk into the Honda and drops into the bucket seat.

We head through a canopy of trees. "You've missed the wisteria," she announces.

"I know. I remember."

"I suppose you do. How many years since you left?"

"About 30." I hope she won't start laying on the guilt.

She doesn't. "I think your family's been better off. I'll be glad to see them."

A feeling of peace passes through me along with the breeze wafting through the windows I have opened to air out the musty car. There were years when Mother made no attempt to hide her disapproval that we'd added five children to the clan.

Shortly after we arrive at her apartment, a medical supply firm rep rings the buzzer. He wheels the big oxygen tank we had ordered into

Mom's bedroom. It squats beside her recliner and soon begins to expel an occasional wheeze.

When I turn on the TV, Mother taps the remote to bring up *Oprah* and says, "I'm so glad to be home." She pulls the recliner handle to raise her legs, then covers them with her rose colored afghan and pats her lap with satisfaction. I'm grateful that I have arrived to bring her some contentment.

That was three days ago. Now, we sit in silence on her patio where the fragrance of new-mown grass blends with the exhaust fumes of cars slowing to turn into the nearby shopping center. Yvonne, a neighbor, rounds the corner with her watering can. I've been hoping some neighbors would drop by. "How about some coffee, Yvonne? Or maybe some lemonade?" I ask.

Yvonne shakes her thick, dark hair. She waves her arm from side to side and sprinkles Mother's philodendron.

"I've lived too long," Mother announces.

"Doris, you must be brave. You are the matriarch. You must set the example." Her neck bent, Yvonne continues across the lawn with her watering can. Even on this hot day, she's dressed all in black.

Later, I meet Yvonne in the laundry where she is counting quarters. She looks up. "Your mother has had a long, full life. As for me, I cut my husband's hair." She taps the washer. "I use this washing machine, but I take the laundry to another dryer. It costs less. Here it costs a fortune." She feeds quarters into the coin slot and shoves it with her palm. "Doris takes these trips to Maine, but all she ever brings us is maple syrup. She is selfish." Yvonne is a bit of a curmudgeon, but she manages to be funny and

I appreciate the help she has given Mom. Poor Yvonne, she works hard to pinch pennies. Mom had a lush life by comparison, yet Yvonne endures her complaining. No wonder she resents Mother's descriptions of her life in China with eight servants and her years in New York studying art at Columbia.

"Would you like her philodendron?" I ask.

"No. It is poisonous."

Yvonne is just one of Mom's neighbors who run errands for her. They visit and bring food. Cookie and I should do something for them. Maybe we can sneak a few curios from Mother's cabinet without her noticing. Yet we haven't planned, and Cookie refuses to discuss anything but Jody's wedding. She's stalling to stay in charge. She and her husband. Actually it's Dennis who's in charge. Dennis, years older than Cookie, had a tough Depression-era childhood. He largely supported his Irish mother and sister with his paper route after their father died. He had to take out bank loans to pay for his engineering degree. Once he'd paid off that debt, his mother got sick. Dennis sent money home every month while his sister cared for their mother, but after she died, his sister got the house. He never got over that. Cookie told me he'd been furious. "We got screwed," he'd said. "This isn't going to happen to us again."

He seems to feel he's entitled to some kind of reparations, because his sister tricked him, but I'm Cookie's sister, not his. On their last trip to Maine, Dennis had ordered me out of the cottage.

"I'll go because of your heart,' I'd said. But you don't own this place, Dennis."

Now that I'm here, some of these puzzle pieces are coming together.

I'd go talk to Cookie this afternoon, but LC Rogers, another neighbor, is coming for tea. Mother had me polish the entire silver tea service because LC is old Greensboro. Her family homestead is in the National Historic Register. Old families still intimidate Mother. She's offered LC a book on the Maine coast because LC's son, Carter, a yachtsman, plans to spend the summer in Maine operating a cruise boat.

LC sails in, settles on the couch and spreads her flowered skirt with her fingertips. She opens a photo album filled with photos of Carter and his bikini-clad girlfriends in Barbados. "He'll be here for three weeks. He'll be taking cruise boats out of Bar Harbor."

"He won't see many bikinis in Bar Harbor," Mother says.

Abruptly LC claps the album shut. "My daughter died, you know."

Mother points to the tube in her nose. "I'm on this oxygen all the time now."

"Oh. I hadn't noticed." LC cranes her neck and squints. "That's terrible. You don't want that. Get a second opinion."

Mother closes her eyes.

LC charges ahead. "My sister's in a nursing home, but I don't get out to see her. It's not on the bus line. Besides, it's terrible." She twists her brooch. "One thing you'd better not have if you've got one is a living will. Tear it up. They'll just use it to kill you. I sat and watched my other sister dying in the nursing home for five days while they did nothing." She leans forward and whispers, "They wouldn't even let her have a glass of water."

33

"Oh, they must have given her water." Mother slides a pillow behind her back.

I take LC's teacup. "Let me just fill this for you. It's Darjeeling." I probably should have served sweet tea, a southern custom.

"No water at all," declares LC.

I pass the cookie plate. "Won't you try one? Please. We can't possibly eat them all."

LC takes two. "All because of that living will. So tear yours up. They're terrible."

Mother traces the veins on her hand. "I carry mine in my purse. I guess I'd better tear it up."

"When is your son coming?" I place the cookies, redolent with cinnamon, on the table beside LC. The smell of the cinnamon reminds me of baking cookies with my kids. I'd give them spoons and they would gather around the bowl to lick the batter. Today, warnings seem to raise fears of salmonella poisoning.

"I don't know where my son is," says LC. "He's out on a boat and he can't call me, but when I see him, I have to get him to change his burial arrangements. He says he's going to give his body to medical science. I want him to be buried in the family plot on top of his daddy and his sister." Now, that begs the imagination.

"I'm going to be cremated and be next to my husband in Maine," Mother says matter-of-factly.

"I'm thinking of doing the same thing. Have you seen what they charge?" LC rubs her fingers across the nubby cover of the Barbados album. "My daughter's buried in our family plot. She didn't want to be buried in Pennsylvania where she died after seventeen months of marriage. Up there they stack you like cordwood." Again, I envision stacked bodies. I try to think of baking cookies or just about anything instead.

"Uh, that Wellspring grocery is such a lovely market," I say. "Their produce is so colorful."

LC appears to notice me for the first time. "It's too expensive. The Yankees patronize it and drive up the prices."

"LC is negative," Mother says as we navigate toward her bedroom after the tea party.

Good thing I can't stay long, or I'd be driving LC around too. I should give Cookie more credit for taking on Mom's care. It gets you down.

I help Mom into bed. She curls into a ball and stays that way until I bring our dinner. Meatloaf, mashed potatoes, and peas -- everything soft and easy to digest. With all this talk about death, it's hard to think up meals. We watch the news and listen to the water swish through the oxygen tank.

"Turn on *Antiques Road Show*," Mother says after dinner. "I'd like to be on that show with my Chinese ancestor chairs. They're very valuable."

"They are stunning."

"What are all these pills for, I wonder?"

I squeeze my eyelids. Some things Mom forgets, but her wary mind holds on to long-term memories. I must ply her for more stories about my father's life, but her mood must be receptive. That is tough to gauge. I hesitate too much.

Today, for what it's worth, I helped her say goodbye to her neighbors. I wish she would show more interest in her life, but at least she isn't trying to gather all of us under the same tombstone. I celebrate little victories. Today I learned that my real father was actually driving the car in which he died.

The days are so choppy. Interruptions tire Mother, I can see it in her eyes. The church calls to ask for her pledge. Cookie drops by every day to see if I'm killing Mom or stealing her artifacts. She always wears those black ballet slippers as if she'd like to study ballet. I don't blame Cookie. Her movements are graceful and deft. I wonder if she is disappointed that Jody dropped dance in middle school in favor of soccer and basketball.

It's crazy. I should be the one checking up on Cookie. For years our parents kept all their papers – their lifelong taxes and cancelled checks – in a big black trunk covered with stickers from their travels. Dad used to pull up a chair and bend over that trunk as he pulled out stacks of rubber-banded check stubs, years and years of them. Mother handles finances well, but Dad was a keeper. He saved everything and kept it in order. At times I used to feel I should ask permission before I tossed anything into the wastebasket.

Cookie must have emptied that trunk when she took over Mother's finances. Maybe that's where she got the list of my father's buildings. Actually, since she and Dennis go to such lengths to keep me away from Mother, I'm beginning to suspect they may have had that list for years. Since Mother asked for it, Cookie and Dennis may have taken that list away from her. I know there's something about my real father in there and I'm the only one who doesn't know what it is. It's eating at me. I don't like these thoughts, but it's hard to think of another reason. Could it be that they are trying to find something I'm supposed to inherit, so they

36

can lay claim to the Maine property? Is it mere spite? Why keep information about my father from me?

One afternoon at Cookie's house, I say, "I'd like to see that list of my father's buildings that Mother mentioned." There, I said it.

Cookie slides into the kitchen and leans toward Dennis. He's wearing his striped apron with the big fish in the middle, stirring basil-scented spaghetti sauce on the stove. It barely reaches around his waist to tie in the back. In spite of his bulk, Dennis moves adroitly. "She wants to see the papers," Cookie whispers.

"Where are they?" I ask. Cookie doesn't realize I've followed.

"You're paranoid." Dennis keeps stirring.

Cookie spins around. "It's all a big mess." She waves her hands dismissing the subject. "Later on. After the wedding."

Dennis points to the cupboard. "Get me a container, Cookie. We'll send some of this sauce back to Doris. She loves my homemade spaghetti sauce. This batch has Roma tomatoes and fresh basil."

If I pursue this, Dennis will take it out on Cookie. It's none of his damn business. I stare at Cookie, knowing they'll edit any papers before I ever see them, but maybe I'm pushing too hard. Intellectual Cookie is neither an extrovert nor a big party giver. Right now she and Dennis are handling all these wedding details along with the responsibility for Mother's affairs. Here I am trying to dredge up ancient history of little concern to either one of them. But this could involve money. The power of attorney has gone to Cookie's head. Still, this is no time to put Mother in the middle of a legal battle that will not only tear the family apart, but also cost more than it's worth.

It's all so draining. So, like Mother, I try to focus on the coming family reunion. At the same time, my anger builds. Yvonne is right. Mom is selfish. What right does she have to tell Cookie and Dennis things about my real father that I don't know?

She's at their mercy now, yet everything is still about Mother. Her power. Her control. She withholds the truth even though she's often too weak to care. I have to skirt around the edges, because somehow I've become the odd woman out here. Mom played the martyr, so long-suffering, when Dad was sick. He turned morose and withdrew. She'd come back from the nursing home and complain, "Old, sick people turn so selfish. They forget that anyone else has any kind of life." Will I be this way when I get old?

One morning I try to dip into genealogy. I open a family tree book I found at the local bookstore and point to the tree's many branches. Mother grew up in Canada. She used to tell me that her father played the violin. I write that on one branch. When I ask about her mother, she says, "My mother told me to get out of Canada. She wanted me to make something of myself."

Once again, I feel her unspoken reproach. I neither married a rich man, nor had a successful career after graduating from Smith. My accomplishment has been the challenge and joy of raising five children. My office jobs have been drudgery by comparison, but they have enabled me to focus primarily on my family.

Mother picks up the newspaper. "Let the dead have their rest. They've earned it." She hunches over the stock quotes with a magnifying glass, sending me the same old message. Her assets are her interest. My origins are none of my business.

She wants to look nice for the wedding. Her creams, her lotions, her makeup rest on a tray table in the bathroom. She has picked out her best outfits for the rehearsal dinner and the wedding. She is determined to leave her oxygen at home.

Then at breakfast she asks, "Why don't you go home?"

"I'm staying so you can live here until after the wedding."

She gives me a look that says 'I don't care if I ever see you again,' and throws her spoon on the table. "I can stay here myself. What am I going to do with my furniture?" She is already offering everything to everyone. She gave the cleaning woman her sterling candelabra.

"Don't worry, we'll work that out."

She tries a deep breath. The oxygen tank sighs. "Oh well, I don't care about possessions."

Neither do I. I just wish I could help her breathe.

The doorbell chimes. "Get that."

It is the physical therapist. A new one again. She crosses the hall and pauses at the edge of the rug. She fingers her long braid. "Hello, Doris. I'm here to help you with some exercises."

"Oh. Is this the day you come?" Mother tries to clear the phlegm from her throat. She pushes out of her chair and turns toward her bedroom, raising her walker before her like a shield. "How I've sacrificed. I've tried so hard," she wails.

From the living room I listen to the polyester swish of the therapist's uniform as she helps Mother into bed. "Doris. You must be thankful for ninety years of good health."

I hear the crackle of Mother's bones as the therapist bends and straightens them.

"You have a remarkable range of motion," the therapist says. "These exercises will help you." She advises Mother to stretch, to walk, to build up her strength for the wedding.

"Well, yes. Maybe I can do that."

The exercises exhaust her. Mom's struggle for life exhausts both of us. I bring up happier times — her travels to China, Manila, Indonesia — the exotic ports where she found her treasures. Maybe it is time for the Prozac, but not all the time.

Beginning to let go, she draws into herself like an old dog trying to head into the woods to die. My mother didn't want to move to Cookie's house, but now that I'm asking questions she's telling me to go home. Soon I will leave and Mom will be forced to live with Cookie and Dennis. This is the way it must be.

The therapist walks into the living room. "I gave your mother a good workout. She's gone to sleep." She hands me a sheet of paper. "See if you can get her to try these exercises."

"Thank you, I will."

2. Cookie Allows

A year and a half after Mother's death, Cookie and I linger over breakfast in Greensboro. The floor-to-ceiling walnut cabinets in Cookie's remodeled kitchen allow her granite counters to remain clutter-free. I shift my gaze out the kitchen window where a butterfly with black wingtips grazes the purple stalk of a butterfly bush that waves in the breeze. The graceful sight calms me as I consider how to bring up the subject of my father's buildings without sounding critical.

Before I can speak, Cookie hands me a binder of onionskin papers, yellowed with age. Secured at the top by a metal clip, the binder is backed by a thin piece of wrinkled cardboard, crisscrossed with tape. "Here's a list of your father's debts," she says.

A thick sheaf of legal-sized papers, their edges curled and torn, hangs out the bottom of the binder. Across the first page Mother had written, *Hans Pederson Estate*. I stare at these papers. I do not speak. I cannot speak. My eyes blur.

"The list of buildings Hans Pederson left me," Mother had called them. "The list of your father's debts," my half-sister has just announced. Whatever they are, they pertain to my real father at the time of his death.

A burning smell wafts from the toaster as an English muffin pops up. Cookie butters both halves, puts them on a plate, and whirls around to set them before me.

"No thank you." I shove the plate back at her. Even though our distant formal family has never been strong on communication, Cookie's secrecy strikes me as blatant theft. I press the binder to my chest and take the stairs to the guest room two at a time. I sit on the bed and zigzag my finger through the tufted hobnails on the white spread. Strong feelings well up inside of me. I don't even know what they are. A few blocks away, the morning train rumbles by.

I brush the fragile pages of my father's estate. My hand shakes. These pages might crumble. I have to get out of here. I throw my belongings into my suitcase, yank up the handle, and bump the suitcase down the stairs, enjoying the rackety clatter the wheels make on each step. With my left hand, I press the papers to my heart, because this is the closest I have ever been to my father.

Her back to me, Cookie loads the breakfast dishes into the dishwasher.

"Is this what Mother called the list of buildings Hans Pederson left her that day in her apartment before the wedding?"

Cookie keeps on loading, her grey-sweatered back hunched over the top rack of the dishwasher. "I don't remember that."

Liar, liar, pants on fire, hang your pants on a telephone wire. The old refrain pops into my head. "The hell you don't."

"Your father was just some wheeler-dealer," she calls over her shoulder as I slam the kitchen door on the way to my car.

I spend three days driving home, staying with friends along the way. I keep my father's papers with me, but neither mention them, nor look at them as I reminisce with classmates about our college years. I can't deal with this while I'm plowing up the interstate. I try to focus on the early fall foliage -- orange and red accents peeking from the green leaves like bright scarves. By the time I reach Maine, the colorful display has reached its peak.

I pore through the papers once I get home. They list rent receipts for an astonishing number of Seattle properties along with charges for repairs, taxes, maintenance, and legal fees. These records are interspersed with letters from Mother's attorneys describing the difficulty of selling Pederson's properties and paintings -- some so large as to be suitable only for a hotel lobby. There seem to be several executors for his estate. Letters signed by Mother, but written in the formal business style I recognize as Dad's, record years of drawn-out negotiations from 1933 to 1941.

Did Mother lie to me about this man? His death in a car accident must have been a shock. Eventually I figure out that he hadn't left her penniless. She'd made no secret of the fact that she had her own money. She'd also made it clear that she didn't want to talk about Hans Pederson.

At least not until that day in her apartment when she'd asked Cookie where these papers were. For a moment, as we clashed again about owning the cottage, she must have wanted me to see them. But instead, Cookie and Dennis held me off until a year and a half after her death.

Now I want to know why she'd stiffened at every mention of my father. He must have been some kind of low life, yet it looks as if I'll never learn what kind. What else did Cookie know? What else did she remove from our mother's apartment before I showed up against her wishes to spend a month with Mom?

I put the papers aside. The deceit and secrecy that lie behind them override any desire I might have to learn more about my real father, Hans Pederson. A blank hole opens. I feel like one of those photos of an Alzheimer's patient – a photo where part of the victim's face disappears behind a smoky haze. Someday maybe I'll blow that smoke away. But not yet. I can't deal with it yet.

I rake leaves, but mostly go through my days in slow motion. Stark skeletons of maples, immovable against the changing light, record the journey of the sun as it sinks lower in the sky. The air chills. Tired all the time, I lack focus until one gray November day, I drive south again to visit my son, Ben, who has moved to Charlotte, North Carolina to build decks. Somehow he's always had a knack for carpentry, so he's settled in a thriving area where he can build a future.

Cookie asks me to stop in Greensboro on the way. She has something for me. I wind through her neighborhood of stately homes, turn into her driveway and park by the brick terrace. Noir, her black lab, sounds a welcoming bark and rubs his head against me as Cookie opens the door.

"Noir is a sweetheart," I say, "and a leader. The last time I took him for a walk, he grabbed his end of the leash and walked *me*."

"Yes. He's an alpha dog all right. He's the boss of our household." Cookie leads the way into the kitchen and pours the usual cup of coffee. "I have something for you." She sets another brittle piece of paper, brown with age, before me. "Here's your adoption record."

Oh no. Here we go again. Must she dispense this new piece of my life like a piece of dessert candy? The adoption record is simple enough, Mother once told me she'd married Dad in 1935 when I was two, but the message here is that Dad didn't adopt me until 1941 when I was eight. I look up. "Why are you giving this to me now?"

She pours cream into her coffee and stirs it slowly and methodically. Noir whines and scratches the kitchen door. She rises quickly and grabs his leash. "I'd better take him out."

She'll have a tantrum like Mother if I push her. Go on about how much of her valuable time she's giving up to serve as executor and how I don't appreciate it. She'll make up some lie. She's hoarding her power, dragging out the settlement of Mother's estate. I'm letting it go, because she's said she'll sell me her half of the Maine cottage after everything's settled. I'll bet Dennis is behind this. The longer the settlement takes, the longer we'll keep sharing the cottage. He lost one house to his sister. I know he doesn't want to lose another one to me. Still, after all these secret shenanigans, our families need a break from each other.

Once I get home, I again put the confusing papers aside. My blood pressure takes off. Through the years I've wondered about my real father now and then, but not that often. I've had a rich family life of my own. Now I realize that by saying nothing and withholding my father's records, Mother, Cookie, and Dennis have robbed me of half my identity.

None of this bothered me before I knew about it. I remember Dad fondly as my loving stepfather, but I just learned that he waited eight years before he adopted me. That hurts. I can't help it. Now, my life feels like a festering sore. All of a sudden, I feel driven to learn about this distant, unpleasant-sounding father from Seattle -- my birthplace a continent away. I have no idea how to do this, but I must, because if anyone should know about this Scandinavian-sounding man, it should be me.

Cookie must have taken those papers out of our parents' big black trunk and confronted Mother about them when she emptied it. I picture Mother undergoing my half-sister's grilling. What did Cookie learn? Probably not much. Both of them are experts at covering their tracks. Mother would have exploded; carried on about her sacrifices to guarantee that Cookie never asked again. Cookie did finally give those papers to me. Maybe our mother told her to let me have them after she was gone.

Move on, I tell myself, it's too late. The estate will be settled. I won't have to deal with Cookie after she sells me the cottage. The days grow short. The nights grow cold. It's dark by four o'clock. I file out of the office with my coworkers, all of us wearing blank expressions as we begin the transition to the long evening ahead.

Still, every now and then I return to the fragile binder of ancient papers. I leaf through the lists -- pages and pages of buildings, apartments, farms, businesses, and the figures to maintain them as they were sold. Plenty of bookkeeping and management for those lawyers through the years -- those hard luck Depression-lingering years from 1933-1941. It comes to me that even though my father died with debts, along with practically everyone else at that time, it was only after he had lived his life not only as a successful businessman, but also as a tycoon. Yes. He must have been an actual tycoon.

I finally realize that one reason nothing makes sense is that 35 of the 233 pages have been carefully torn out of the binder. Many seem to have been the first pages of Mother's letters from her Seattle attorneys, Padden and Moriarty. Who removed those pages? Why? Perhaps the missing pages showed that along with the debts and claims against my father's properties, he'd also had assets. Cookie says she didn't do it. Why, after saving my father's papers for 55 years, would Mother have torn out 35 pages? Cookie had said that my father was 'just some wheeler-dealer.' Maybe he was a crook. A thug. Maybe Mother didn't want me to know that my father was a Seattle robber baron.

These papers have raised more questions than answers.

Who were my parents?

Who am I?

3. Old Papers

In 2003, four years after Mother's death, I sit in my attorney's office in Maine on a breezy May day as we complete my purchase of the summer cottage our parents built when Cookie and I were children. After four more years of wrangling, the two of us have finally reached this point. I know it's a sad decision for Cookie's family, especially since Dennis felt cheated when he lost his mother's house, but he's getting a good deal this time. We're paying dearly. I don't mind, it's worth it. It just doesn't work for two clashing sisters and their seven grown children to share vacation property. Cookie had held me off for years, probably ever since they'd taken possession of my father's papers. It still rankled, the way they'd tried to keep me away from Mother before Jody's wedding. I remember the exact conversation.

The same evening Mother had told me she'd moved to my half-sister's house, Cookie had called. "There's no need for you to come so early. We've brought a few things, and her oxygen tank is here now."

"But that room you've put her in is right in the middle of all the wedding commotion. Doorbells. UPS trucks."

"She's settled now. The tank can't be moved. Here. Talk to her."

Mother had picked up her amplified receiver. "Don't come. We don't want you."

They had the upper hand. I was the stepdaughter with the renegade father. Since I'd always considered myself the family bastard, I generally avoided control issues. But by then, Cookie had assumed more control over Mother than Mother had ever exerted over us. I couldn't let her do it. I called the oxygen people. "Can the tank be moved?"

"Of course. It goes wherever the patient wants it."

As soon as I'd given Mom the option, she was thrilled to go back to her own apartment. I'm so glad I went and spent that last month with her. Whenever I think I'm making too big a deal out of Cookie holding back the papers, I remember the lies. It's sad. It hurts.

———

Now the estate is settled. My half-sister and I can stop resenting each other and get on with our lives. I have to give Cookie credit for one thing though -- she did give me those papers. She could have kept them and pretended Mother had never mentioned them -- except we both knew that she had.

My attorney's tall, nineteenth-century office window frames the blooming lilacs beside the granite monument on the town common. Etched on that monument are the names of the town's warriors from the American Revolution through the Vietnam War. Descendants of these families still fish, farm, and build boats along Maine's nearly four thousand miles of coast. I belong here. Dad's old Maine family adopted me into their clan, and I've assumed their Colonial New England heritage even though it isn't mine by birth.

The lawyer assembles the legal papers for the cottage purchase into neat piles, squaring them with the edges of his hands. I finger the brittle pages of my father's estate settlement in my lap. Hoping they might contain clues to my lineage, however disgraceful it might be, I reach across the desk and hand him the papers. "This is all I know about my father," I say. "I wish I knew more."

He flattens his palms on the desk and slowly spreads his fingers, then moves his index finger across a line on the first page. "Here is the probate number of his will. Go find someone to look it up at the King County Courthouse in Seattle."

Out the window I observe a flock of seagulls soar across the common, wings outstretched as they float on air currents toward the Kennebec River. Their raucous cries announce that they have something to say. My growing sense of wonder leaves me, once again, speechless.

"Okay. I'll do it," I finally manage.

I leave the office half an hour later, slide into my Saturn car, and head northeast on Route One. At the turnoff for the peninsula, I relax against the seat and notice how spring has come to Maine with a speed that awes the senses. The blazing green of budding maples gives way to fragrant marsh grass at the river bend beside the mudflats exposed by an outgoing tide. A flock of eider ducklings surge protectively around their ducklings as I pass a cove. I pull into my driveway. The sun seems to wash the shingles like a cloth scrubbing winter away. I have just bought a cottage. Perhaps I will now find a father.

"Do you know anyone who does this kind of research?" I ask Don, a childhood friend from Maine who lives in Seattle, when I call him about the papers.

"I don't, but I'll take a stab at it. I know where that courthouse is. It's downtown, just above Pioneer Square."

Knowing very little about my father at this time, I knew virtually nothing about Pioneer Square; aptly named because Seattle pioneers created this area from the tide flats to expand the city's narrow waterfront. Like early settlers everywhere, they filled it with debris -- sawdust, wood pilings, gravel, and fire rubble with no concept or concern for what changes time and tide would bring. I soon learned that much of my father's work took place in this area.

Don spends the better part of a day at the courthouse. He finds the death certificates and wills for Hans Pederson and his wife, Marie.

When I see his manila envelope in my mailbox a few days later, I clutch it like a starving animal, race into the cottage, and turn off the phone. Shoving my feet under a cushion on the window seat, I ease the papers out of the envelope; slowly, slowly, my curiosity mixed with fear.

The grainy courthouse copies of the Pedersons' death certificates tell me that my father's wife, Marie, died of diabetes in March 1932, at the age of sixty-two. Hans died of a cerebral hemorrhage resulting from years of hypertension, on September 6, 1933, shortly after his sixty-ninth birthday. Since I was born on August 9, 1933, this meant that he died when I was twenty-eight days old. As I suspected, he had neither been run down by a car nor blinded by early-morning sunshine as he drove one himself. Don also includes a copy of my father's March 1933 will. It states

52

that since his wife, 'Dorris' (my mother), is expecting a child, he intends to leave his assets to her. His will was drawn one year after Marie died. Five months before I was born.

So. They had actually been married. I had always wondered. So had Cookie. One time she'd said, "I always thought you were illegitimate." We'd never talked about it. It seemed like such a disgrace. Well, Hans Pederson might have left my poor mother penniless, but at least she could hold her head up as a widow, not a mistress. At least I wasn't the product of a one-night stand. Still, they couldn't have been married for long. And my mother's name was Doris, with only one r. Not Dorris. Why hadn't my father known how to spell her name?

All my life my mother had lied to me about this man, and now she was gone. The clues Don has sent me from the King County Courthouse are enough to get me started on my search for the truth. I try to remember anything Mother might have said about my father. Nothing comes to mind. Whatever he did, I want to know about it. It can't hurt anyone now.

With the date of my father's death in hand, I call the *Seattle Post Intelligencer* and ask for his obituary. Soon another dark and speckled photocopy from a sixty-seven-year old newspaper arrives. My eye is drawn to the bottom of the page, an ad for newspaper home delivery. A boy wearing a three-piece suit, knee socks and knickers, vest, tie, and tam-o'-shanter hat, tosses a newspaper at a house as he rides by on his bike. Evidently newsboys dressed this way at the time of my birth in 1933.

Above the ad, the heartbreaking photo of my father against a black background portrays the puffy face and miserable expression of a very sick man. His high blood pressure must have led to kidney failure. Fluid rounds his chin. It fills his eyelids and cheeks. His sad mouth turns down; his hair and mustache seem mangy. The photo must have been taken shortly before his death. Maybe it looks this way because the page is so old.

The obituary reads:

"... Pederson, pioneer Seattle contractor and a veteran of the Alaska gold rush, died yesterday morning in his home on Queen Anne Hill, in one of the many apartment houses he leaves behind as monuments to his success.

... He established himself as the first plaster contractor in the city and then branched out into general contracting. He built the addition to the County-City building, the Arctic Club, and before the Depression he owned thirty-nine apartment houses of his own construction in the city.

He is survived by his recent bride and an infant daughter, Paula; and two sisters and a brother in Denmark."

How could that sick and broken-down old man have done all those things? How could he have been my father?

I run my hand through Frosty's thick coat. A Samoyed, Frosty belongs to an Arctic breed used as sled dogs in Alaska. Having once read that Eskimos made garments from Samoyed fur, I'd brushed bags full of Frosty's fur and taken it to a woman at the farmer's market to spin into yarn when I'd first moved to Maine. Then I knit a Frosty-fur sweater, soft as Angora, for our youngest son, Ed, to take to college.

Frosty responds to my touch with a wolf-like howl. Hans Pederson, a veteran of the Alaska gold rush, might have mushed across the frozen tundra with a team of sled dogs like Frosty. I too, had chosen an arctic dog. My Scandinavian father left Denmark for the Pacific Northwest. I left New Jersey and immersed myself in Maine's bracing climate, filled with fish and forests.

I read the obituary several times before I notice that my name, Paula, is listed at the bottom, while my mother, Doris, is mentioned only as "his recent bride." Could it be that she began to distance herself from her husband as soon as he died? I was born only a little over a year after my father's first wife had died. His friends may not have happily received Mom.

I try to picture my mother in Seattle. On her own mother's advice, she told me she'd left the family farm in Alberta and struck out alone for Seattle, USA. A beauty, she'd once been chosen Miss Edmonton. She must have longed for a better life, for pretty clothes, for finer things. While she may have found Seattle more sophisticated than Edmonton, she moved sometime during the Depression. The section of Seattle called "Skid Road," the path where oxen once pulled newly-cut logs from the hillside, had evolved into the slum of "Skid Row," filled with "Hoovervilles," malodorous waterfront shanties pieced together from scrap wood, tin, and cardboard; homes for the down and out. So far away from home, Mother must have been terrified that she'd end up in some flimsy Hooverville hovel, wet and chilled in Seattle's gray dampness.

Then she met this rich widower -- elderly, yes — in the elevator of an apartment building. He had just lost his wife. In a short time, he wanted to marry her. Why not? She must have been frantic when he died

55

so soon, leaving her with a tiny baby. She knew nothing about his complex business affairs. She must have wondered, as she did so often in her life, *what will people think?*

From now on I will be a detective. I will fit the puzzle pieces together. I begin a search.

"He's listed in Bagley and Hanford," a reference librarian tells me when I call the Seattle public library. Clarence Bagley's 1916, *History of Seattle from the Earliest Settlement to the Present Time*, and C.H. Hanford's 1924, *Seattle and Environs*, feature biographies of the pioneers who built the city.

My father's stolid photo regards me from the facing page of Hanford's article. I see a dignified, broad-shouldered man in shadow against a black background. His visible eye, large and determined, stares straight ahead; his stern expression, white hair, round white collar and half his face the only relief against the blackness.

He was already more than fifty years old when Bagley's history was published. Reaching my father's house, the dairyman would have stepped from a horse-drawn wagon and looped the reins over the hitching post before leaving the eggs, butter and cheese on the back stoop along with the milk, its thick cream ringing the top of the glass bottle. Strong men would have hoisted blocks of ice with tongs from the sawdust-covered floors of larger wagons, wrestled the ice into the kitchen, and placed it inside the wooden icebox. So long ago, so far away, yet I begin to feel a kinship, because I see in myself my father's straight nose and thick white hair.

Bagley notes that my father constructed many of Seattle's streets and public buildings by combining utility with beauty of design. He writes: *"A man of high principles and more than ordinary ability, Mr. Pederson enjoys the trust of all with whom he has had business relations and is generally conceded to be one of the foremost factors in the promulgation of Seattle's greatness."* I feel proud. Yet my mother denied his memory.

Bagley's stilted language went along with the buttoned-up Victorian clothes. My father was surely no struggling young architect who left Mother penniless with me to raise. But why had she so angrily changed the subject whenever I mentioned him?

My search halts after the Seattle librarian refers me to the state library in Olympia. Their building is closed for repairs in the aftermath of the 2001 Nisqually earthquake. Also known as "The Ash Wednesday Earthquake," the 6.8 earthquake's epicenter was in Puget Sound, but the shock extended to neighboring states Oregon and Idaho and into Canada to the north.

The library repairs take a while, so I settle into winter with another project. A local builder agrees to remodel the Maine cottage. He needs indoor work to get through the winter months and our place has an existing roof. I plan to gut the fifty-six-year-old interior, replace the wiring, reconfigure the rooms, and add a 12x12 bedroom. Now, like my father, I will be a general contractor.

Our dirt road is plowed in January. Frosty tunnels through drifts that rise in November and stay until April. A layer of ice on the bay rises and falls with the ten-foot tides and spreads toward the distant islands. Chip and I can't stay away. We park the car in the small oval cleared by the plow and step into our snowshoes. Leaning forward, Chip leads the way across the causeway, his ratty old ski sweater rising up his long back, revealing aged long johns, gray and stretched. He wears the hat I knit him to cover his thinning hair. Chip hates to waste money on clothes. Each afternoon we sweep the sawdust after the carpenters leave. We load the trunk of the Saturn with scrap lumber, drywall, and brick from the old chimney and haul it to the dump.

Like many rural dumps, ours is a community center. Politicians stump at the dump, competing with the thud of salvage hunters tossing lumber and scrap metal into truck beds. Whatever hasn't sold at yard sales -- bikes, toys, wobbly-legged chairs -- gets left at the swap shed. You hear the old saying, "Use it up, wear it out, make it do, or do without." Good old New England thriftiness at its best.

That winter my anger keeps me warm as I comb through the cottage and toss one thing after another of my mother's. She had deceived me. I'd been a coward. A wimp. Out go the fussy bridge table covers edged with gold braid. Then I cradle the graceful antique pitcher with the gold handle that Dad and I bought for Mother on a trip to Nova Scotia. Some memories are worth keeping.

I pack the flatware in a box. The monogrammed scrolling 'P' on the silver-plated knife is flaking off, revealing dark metal beneath. I remember the evening I dried the knife after dinner and asked Mom, "Where did this come from?"

A guttural sound of disgust had emerged from her throat. "It was your father's." She'd grabbed the knife from me and thrown it in the drawer. I'll keep that flaking silver, but I feel like smashing the Noritake china, a gift from one of their Japanese friends. Since I can't stand the sight of it, I box it and leave it at the swap shed.

The manager of the dump, officially the transfer station, keeps the china in her warming hut. She spreads the word that the graceful flowered dishes are available on loan to anyone giving a nice party. One of these days maybe I'll borrow them myself.

Today, I wish Mother could come to her remodeled cottage with its open floor plan and built-in window seat spread with cheerful cushions. She was always embarrassed when people visited the old dark summer camp. She'd apologize for our gloomy kitchen and our cramped quarters. Everyone else, everyone else's home, everyone else's things were invariably better than ours. I always wanted to protect her, except for the times that she apologized for me.

4. Burning and Building

The Washington State library in Olympia finally reopens after completing their earthquake renovations. Along with a bill for thirty dollars, they send me a treasure trove of articles about Hans Pederson from their archives. I will never believe the Internet should supplant libraries, the repositories of our civilization, our history, and our culture.

So I continue to meet my father through old news stories. Born in 1864 to a farm family on the Isle of Fyn in Denmark, he emigrated to the U.S. when he was twenty, during the tumultuous years when the Scandinavian countries found themselves with more farmers than farmland, more job seekers than jobs. He joined a boatload of emigrants to America in 1884, and soon arrived in Minnesota. There he became part of the horde of Scandinavians willing to farm and log forests for a wage low enough to drive away the locals. A Minnesota friend once told me that her parents kept a book of state history on the living-room coffee table. In one old photo of a logging camp, the foreman states, "On my crew I have but one white man and fifty Swedes."

Too ambitious to stay in any of Minnesota's established Scandinavian settlements, Hans Pederson continued west. He worked his way through the Cascade Mountains to the West Coast with the Northern Pacific Railroad. He tried Los Angeles and San Francisco, headed north to Vancouver, and then back south to Seattle, arriving three years before Washington became the forty-second state in 1889. He joined the throng of construction workers along the mosquito-infested waterfront of Puget Sound, much of it covered by Henry Yessler's swampy sawmill. It rained most of the time. On a sunny day, the sight of Mt. Rainier, sacred to the Indians, surely triggered the same reverence and awe that it does today.

The city grew fast. As it rose into the steep hills, sewage and water flowed downward, reached the flats, then backed up as it met the incoming tide. Toxic mud mounded over weeds, settled around tree stumps, and covered the rutted streets and wooden sidewalks with slime and the stench of brine. Just reading about the early days made me long for a hot shower.

Those pioneering men had to live somewhere. Few women were ready to follow them. At least the flophouses, saloons, and brothels brought camaraderie, comfort and dry feet in the midst of Seattle's ubiquitous gray dampness.

None of my father's biographers associate him with the dark and violent waterfront of Yesler Way where Christian missions were interspersed with "hotels." Many doubled as gambling houses, offering a variety of accommodations behind the saloons. Vast halls held rows of adult "cribs," their boxy sides affording a modicum of privacy for evening revelry. J. Kingston Pierce notes in *Eccentric Seattle* that early prostitutes were often Indians who competed for customers by shampooing their hair with urine. Police "protection" helped fill the city's coffers. The nimble trade put Seattle in the top tier of the white slave business.

News articles report that my father worked hard, saved his meager pay, and wasted no time building his future. In a 1978 article written forty-five years after Pederson's death, Clinton Hyde, Seattle's Danish consular secretary, quoted him as saying, "I came direct from a farm in Denmark. No, I didn't go to school and study engineering. A boy learns to do everything on the farm." Restless and driven, he began a lifelong pattern of working the land as well as the city. Town life was too confining, country life too leisurely.

In 1886, as autumn burned the aspens to fiery gold, my father staked a claim on a 160-acre homestead north of Seattle in Woodinville, settling in the Hollywood Hills with other Scandinavian farmers. They helped each other clear the land and hunt small game. They basked in the knowledge that just beyond their fertile farmland the forest backdrop offered a wilderness to explore and space to expand. My father found a stove in an abandoned camp and carried it six miles home on his back, then lived in a tent until he could raise his house. The next step was to buy a cow, his only company, but when winter came he had to sell her as the land did not suffice for cattle. With little work outdoors during the rainy winter, he enjoyed the "free life" in nature, finding trees and flowers he had never known.

Soon realizing that farm life offered only minimal challenges for his energies, he found learning and fellowship with his stove, his library, and his neighbors who had also been farmers. He took refuge in his book collection -- writings by the Danish author and editor, Henrik Pontoppidan and other good works. American books such as Longfellow's Indian legends taught him the English language.

He was not alone in choosing that lifestyle.

Although Seattle's population of scalawags and reprobates made better copy, the reputedly sober Scandinavians shared a background of hard work in frigid climates, as well as childhoods filled with farm labor, fishing, logging, forests, and boats. Leaving homeland that offered constrained lives of survival, they brought energy and vitality to the west where many had the discipline to save their hard-earned dollars.

My father's wilderness homestead lasted only two years before it burned to the ground. One day, he felled some trees on his property, then left to spend a few days working the railroads. An uneasiness possessed him as he returned and began to smell smoke. Reaching his house, he found that few lumps of earth remained. Not only did he lose his tools and clothes, but also his beloved library. All he had left were the clothes on his strong back.

"I speculated," he reported, "On how the fire could have started and realized I had only myself to blame. See, to clear a forest, one generally drills holes in the fallen tree trunks -- one every ten feet. You fill the holes with petroleum and burn them to break up the trunks so they can be more easily transported. When I made the mistake of leaving my homestead for two days, the trunks must have burned quietly until the wind came up and blew sparks to my house. With all our privacy here, none of the neighbors noticed."

He moved back to town and spent his free time reading in the Seattle Public Library.

Prophetically, my father's Woodinville fire preceded the inferno that engulfed the Seattle waterfront in June of 1889. Five city blocks of wooden buildings along Puget Sound were reduced to blackened trash. Not unusual at a time when oil lamps and candles provided lighting for wooden structures that were also heated by wood stoves. Thousands of men lost their jobs. Those who stayed settled into countless refugee camps that speckled the grass, the muddy blackened streets, and the shores of Lake Washington.

Opportunity arose out of the smoldering rubble. Architects swarmed to Seattle to plan the buildings of stone and brick that soon replaced the rough and stinking wooden structures. Noted architect Elmer Fisher designed Seattle's six-story Pioneer Building, considered so remarkable that upon its completion, the American Institute of Architects labeled it "the finest building west of Chicago." Its roughhewn stone base, arched windows, and Roman archway exemplified the Romanesque revival style in vogue during The Gilded Age. Covering the site of Henry Yessler's swampy sawmill, it is today the architectural standout of Pioneer Square, the restored downtown Seattle oasis with its totem in the central square that symbolizes the city's turbulent past. My father laid the foundation for his business by working on the commercial buildings of brick, masonry, stone, and iron that replaced the original wooden structures that had burned to cinders.

But all that construction turned out to be too much too soon. Four years later, the panic of 1893 ended the frenzied development that marked the Gilded Age. Railroads, mines, hotels, and banks failed. From 1890-1910, Seattle's population increased five-fold to 237,000. Many of the European transplants who had staked their futures on a train ride to the western frontier milled around with little to do. Some resorted to digging clams at low tide on the shores of Puget Sound.

5. A Golden Future

Nimble Seattle took off again in 1897 when word spread that gold had been discovered along the Yukon's Klondike River. The ship *Portland* steamed into port and disgorged prospectors laden with sacks of gold. Front-page headlines carried the news to the East Coast where many men, even if they had found work after the 1893 depression, felt stifled in factory, office or low-paying retail jobs. Here was their chance to tackle the *real* frontier -- a wilderness so vast that anyone could come back a millionaire.

Flyers sent all over world touted Seattle as the gateway to Alaska. Even so, most of those who bolted to the Yukon were Americans or recent immigrants who had left their homelands for such an opportunity. Canny Seattle natives stepped up to supply the prospectors with provisions. By 1898, countless mining firms opened offices in the Pioneer Building. Hotels, theaters, and outfitters sprang up to meet the needs of hordes of miners who fought for space on ships destined for the gold fields. One photo shows a team of nine sled dogs, some probably stolen from their owners' yards, harnessed in single file in front of a scattering of men dressed like train conductors. Signs behind them announce the *Queen City Dancing Academy* and the *Yukon Mining School -- panning, sluicing, rocking & c. by practical Alaska miners.*

"He was among the first to answer the call of the North when the manhood of the world stampeded toward the arctic and the sparkle of gold," notes my father's obituary. He and a partner crammed themselves aboard a ship and joined the throng of prospectors who washed up on Alaskan shores like flotsam on the tides.

He didn't stay long enough to make his fortune. According to Hanford's Seattle and Environs 1852-1924, "After enduring many hardships and dangers, he returned to Seattle poorer in purse, but richer in experience."

What an exciting time! I want to go to Seattle and face the heady choices. I want to go to Alaska and experience the vast, frozen landscape. I want to absorb the drive and ingenuity of my father.

His first big break came in 1904 with the contract to plaster Seattle's first all-steel skyscraper, the Alaska Building, at Second and Cherry Streets. According to Olaf Linck, one of my varied sources, Hans Pederson bought Princess Angeline's entire supply of postcards late one afternoon in front of the Alaska Building.

Alaska Building under construction in 1904 printed with permission from the Museum of History & Industry (MOHAI)

Shortly afterwards, Linck says she shuffled back to her shack on the waterfront near the Pike Place market where she wrapped her shawl tightly around herself and lay down to spend her last night on this earth.

69

Princess Angeline was the eldest daughter of Chief Seattle of the Duwamish tribe, for whom the city was named. The chief sold Seattle to the pioneer white men, left his daughter Kikisoblu with them, and took the rest of his family and his tribe out to a reservation. Mrs. Maynard, a pioneer wife, changed Kikisoblu's name to Princess Angeline in honor of her position. Princess Angeline limped through the city streets with the aid of a cane, enveloped by a shawl and a red kerchief over her head. She wove baskets and sold postcards that bore a photo of her grief-stricken face. She also took in laundry.

Linck's story conflicts with Seattle chronology since Princess Angeline died in 1896 before Pederson had built anything. Perhaps Linck embellished his story to honor Hans Christian Andersen, Denmark's illustrious author. His inclusion of Princess Angeline in his writing about my father, is reminiscent of Andersen's tale, *The Little Match Girl*.

The heartbreaking story describes the plight of a child sent out to sell matches on New Year's Eve. To keep warm, she lights the matches one by one, each time seeing visions of delicacies spread beneath a brightly lit Christmas tree. After the last match burns out, the child slowly freezes to death.

Princess Angeline's sad ending instantly reminded me of that story from the holiday tales of my childhood. By contrast Hans Pederson, newly arrived in Seattle in 1896, was about to see his career take off as the new century arrived.

After he plastered the Alaska Building, he moved his office into Suite 1224 where his listing for a general contractor read "Fireproof Buildings a Specialty." Of course, no one yet knew how high these new steel-framed buildings could rise without toppling. His talent for estimating and bidding soon established his reputation as the contractor who carried his office around in his memory and in a little black book in his pocket. Bagley notes, *"The public soon recognized that he was fair and just in the execution of contracts and that his ingenuity was such as to enable him to wisely direct the labors of those in his employ."*

He hired several hundred men to build the Milwaukee and St. Regis hotels, along with the Pantages, Fox, and Blue Mouse theaters.

Pantages Theatre in 1915 at the NE corner of University St. & 3rd Avenue, Seattle. Renamed the Palomar in 1936, torn down in 1964. Printed with permission from Seattle Museum of History & Industry (MOHAI).

Fox Theater originally the Alhambra Theatre in 1909 printed with permission from Seattle Museum of History & Industry (MOHAI).

He cleared large tracts of land in Skagit and Whatcom counties. He established dairy farms and raised stock in Snohomish County. We have stock certificates from the large grain and fruit farm he operated in California. He built banks and much of Seattle's Chinatown with his partner Goon Dip.

Dip was an important figure in Seattle's development. Goon Dip Young was appointed China's honorary consul to Seattle in 1909. The fact that he and Hans Pederson were partners in developing buildings in Seattle's Chinatown offers hints at Pederson's values and personality. Dip was one of the most influential Chinese on the West Coast in the early 20th Century. This followed a period of acute hostility toward Chinese starting with the severe economic slump that lasted from 1873 to 1879. In language reminiscent of today, Chinese were viewed as "taking our jobs," leading to the Chinese Exclusion Act of 1882. This denied entry to Chinese for 10 years with few exceptions. Dip left the U.S. and returned to China where he married, then returned to the U.S. shortly before the

Act took force. Dip distinguished himself through his courteous personality and obvious ability. When he died in 1933, the *Seattle Daily Times* eulogized him for his "innate courtesy, the kindly philosophy, the 'do unto others' doctrine common to all faiths into his daily life…"

Pederson also worked with Reginald Heber Thomson on one of the most visible and difficult tasks to carve out land in Seattle: The regrades to level steep hills. William Wilson's 2009 book *Shaper of Seattle* describes Thomson's tenure as Seattle City Engineer from 1892-1912 as a time of incredible growth, much of it financed by riches from the gold fields. This period encompassed the construction of railroads and ship canals, Seattle's sewer and water systems, and especially the ambitious regrades. Thomson ordered the hills that rose above the downtown area to be topped off and the land reconfigured to expand the downtown area, locked in a narrow swath of land between the hills and Puget Sound.

Regrades were considered essential for transportation progress. Wilson's book presents a Seattle Municipal Archives chart that shows the horsepower required for difficult grades. At the turn of the twentieth century, one horse could pull a wagon at street level. One of these wagons with huge wheels could deliver ice and groceries to your door. A one-to-four-percent grade required three horses, and a fifteen percent road grade required nine horses. Those nine horses, necks bent, snorting steam, pulled flat-bedded wagons overflowing with sacks and barrels through rutted roads and up rising hills. Drivers and deliverymen in hip boots avoided stomping hooves and swishing tails as they carried sacks and crates on their shoulders through the pervasive drizzle. The regrades did expand the downtown commercial area, but automobiles soon replaced horse-drawn transportation and rendered obsolete the massive 1910 regrades that transformed Seattle.

On a 2014 Seattle trip with a group of friends, our leader, a Seattle resident, took us to the Gates Foundation, the Chihuly Glass Museum, and the Boeing Air and Space Museum. That afternoon, we walked across the wormy piers of the Argosy Cruise docks, scheduled soon to be replaced. Orange construction cones marked the waterfront stores and restaurants that would soon close to enable construction of a tunnel to replace a waterfront viaduct. The project remains in the news.

A December 9, 2014 *New York Times* article states:

"In the latest blow, project engineers said that 30 or more buildings in the historic Pioneer Square area — a staging area for Klondike gold rush miners heading North to Alaska in the late 1800s and now one of the city's premier tourist stops — had unexpectedly settled —

'A whole block just went down an inch," said Todd Trepanier, State transportation official.

Seattle stays wet and the waterfront land base keeps sinking -- slowly, but steadily. For the regrades, veterans of the Klondike gold rush used explosives and hydraulic sluicing water cannons to blow the tops off the hills. In *Skid Road*, Murray Morgan documents the transformation of the hills first logged by the pioneers, and then lopped off by the engineers who washed nearly as much dirt from the downtown hills as was moved during the digging of the Panama Canal. They sent the dirt own the hills to the waterfront to fill in more of the tide flats, thereby adding more trash to the waterfront's ever-shifting base.

Imagine the deafening racket at a time when even normal street commerce included curses, shouts, and whips cracking on the backs of terrified horses. My father worked on the Denny Hill regrade and the construction of the New Washington Hotel, relocated to the newly razed land below it.

Where previously sewage and water had flowed downhill, only to shoot up like geysers beneath the advancing tide, new sewer and water lines created outfalls to the bay, a boon that followed the advent of flush toilets. The plumber Thomas Crapper is often mistakenly credited with this improvement in plumbing design, but his name can only rightly be associated with the function for which it is used. A convoluted trail of patents and folklore connected Crapper's plumbing company with the "waterfall waste remover." The name stuck. Further plumbing improvements included "needle baths" — stalls where one or more showerheads rained clean water on the bather.

Once the streets were leveled, the sidewalks sank on their muddy foundation of sawdust from the old mills, charcoal from the 1889 fire, and soil sluiced from the hills. The pre-fire sidewalks settled to rest anywhere from ten to 32 feet below the new street levels. They had to be raised so the sewage could flow.

The buildings sank. Roofs were raised after the first floors were built. Again the sidewalks sank. The sidewalks were a sideshow. Pedestrians forced to descend ladders from the street to the sidewalk had to cross the mud that sluiced between the raised streets and the sidewalks, and then climb other ladders to enter the second floor of seven-story buildings.

Picture the ladies climbing up and down ladders steadied by eager prospectors and carpenters who peered up their mud-skimming skirts, past their high-button shoes and striped stockings. Sadly, several people died when they fell off ladders onto the sidewalks. A few also drowned in muddy sinkholes. Nobody counted the hapless horses that lost their footing and rolled off the roads to their deaths on the sidewalks.

A second set of sidewalks had to be constructed over the first. My father took the job, leaving his imprint in the sidewalk cement wherever he worked. Today, some partially sunken Seattle sidewalks, like mini-moats beside the buildings, are embedded with cleats for safety and bordered with wrought-iron railings. Clinton Hyde's 1978 article, *"Forgotten Contractor left Imprint in Sidewalks,"* noted Hans Pederson's name etched into the downtown Seattle sidewalks.

Hyde also reported that Pederson was lead contractor in 1916 for the second Arctic Club.

Arctic Building in 1917 at 3rd Avenue and Cherry Streets.
Printed with permission: Museum of History & Industry (MOHAI).

As C.L. Smith and J. Pheasant-Albright explain in their book *Private Clubs of Seattle*, the Arctic Club was constructed as a meeting place for men with business interests in Alaska -- a venue where the city's movers and shakers could socialize in more luxurious settings than the downtown bars and saloons.

The club's lobby and stairway featured Alaskan marble and a stunning second-floor dome room with a ceiling of wired stained glass. Terra cotta walruses surrounding the exterior of the landmark building's third floor, make a striking display to passersby to this day.

© 2016 Wendy Wiley

Club members who gathered under the opulent domed ceiling of the dining room evidently greeted my father, a lifelong member of the club, as "King Hans." I expect his loyalties were torn when, rumor has it, a fight broke out one night between members of the Arctic Club and Alaska Club, the city's first skyscraper that he had plastered in 1904. The two clubs joined forces in 1908, but the rivalry continued even after the second Arctic Club was built. According to fiftieth anniversary club records, the old Arctic Club's wooden bar was removed through a window and installed in the new club. The Arctic Club boasted more than 1,000 members until 1959.

In 1900, at age 26, Hans Pederson married Marie Madsen, a young woman five years his junior, from Lolland, the fourth largest island of Denmark. They wed in the home of the Danish Consul in Seattle. The Pedersons spoke only Danish at home. Marie, never mentioned in the articles, seems to have possessed a business sense as acute as her husband's. In a 1921 directory, her name is listed beside Hans' as a contractor and builder. My father seems to have been attracted to ambitious, risk-taking pioneer women who looked out for themselves. Unlike Hans, Marie had a large family presence in Seattle. Two of her nephews witnessed the will she drew in 1931, a year before she died. During a time of worldwide privation, she bequeathed an incredible $250,000 to 74 friends and relatives of all ages in the closely-knit Seattle Danish community. The Pedersons must have known everyone in town.

In 1908, eight years after their marriage, my father built Washington Hall, a building that provided housing and social space for newly arrived Danish immigrants. For many years it served as the hub of the social and cultural life of Seattle's Danish population. The building, which has evolved in its mission, is still in use after 109 years. Washington Hall has served as a paying arts venue, hosting such performers as Marian Anderson, Billie Holiday, Duke Ellington and Joe Louis. The Historic Seattle Preservation Foundation raised nearly $15 million to restore the building and ensure its continuation as an arts and community facility. A beautiful restoration debuted in 2016.

Following the downtown regrades my father partnered with Goon Dip who convinced his countrymen to move their shops from the Elliott Bay tidelands to the King Street Station area, thereby establishing Chinatown's new location. Pederson worked on the Milwaukee Hotel in 1911 at 668 King Street -- the heart of the new Chinatown where Goon Dip eventually lived in the penthouse. These two immigrant venture capitalists supplied countless jobs for their countrymen. Goon Dip became the largest provider of Chinese labor in the Northwest, finding workers for the many Pacific salmon canneries as far north as Alaska.

Some of the early twentieth century buildings built by these men still serve as a base for the international melting pot that Seattle has become. One of the best examples is Washington Hall. Another surviving testament to their impact is King Street, which is the heart of Seattle's International District referred to as Chinatown. A 2010 Milwaukee Hotel renovation has created apartments that celebrate diversity with residents hailing from Asia, India, Taiwan and the Philippines.

Goon Dip's Milwaukee Hotel penthouse remained his Seattle residence throughout his life. He died there in 1933, six days after Hans Pederson died in his own Narada Apartment penthouse.

Since I had two fathers, I sometimes imagine myself with two mothers as well. As a preschooler in early 20th century Seattle, I'd be wearing one of those little white christening-type dresses and standing next to Marie in her dark feathered hat and shawl as we waited for the streetcar near our home at 1119 Northern. She'd hold me firmly by the hand as we climbed the streetcar step and paid our nickel fare. The streetcar lines directed the city's commercial and housing growth, providing opportunities for Marie's husband, Hans. His apartment buildings and commercial projects helped to provide housing and jobs for Seattle's immigrants, many of them Scandinavian. A pink-cheeked porcelain doll, also wearing an embroidered white dress, would dangle from my other hand as we paused to stand on my father's logo, etched into the sidewalk. We'd watch an organ grinder turning out, "A Bicycle Built for Two." A monkey on a leash, in a little suit and hat, would hold out a tin cup and beg for coins.

The Pedersons had no children of their own. Their adopted son, Hans Jr., a nephew of Marie's, died at 19, while still in high school. Judging by comments in the articles and by my father's prodigious output, he buried his grief in his work. Poor Hans Jr., my father's only hope for an heir, died too young to carry on our father's growing empire.

Enough information. I stop my search. I withdraw. I hide in my condo and look out the window at the gray Maine winter, at the ice and dirty slush that line the driveway. I grieve for my stepbrother who, had he lived, might even have been my father. In that case, my father would have been my grandfather, or possibly my great-grandfather since he was old enough to have been my mother's grandfather. How bizarre.

If only I could have known my father. If only he could have known me, his genetic daughter, for more than 28 days. His example would have inspired me. My mother never encouraged me in school. Her only wish for me was to marry a rich man -- it had worked for her. When after two years at Smith College I had not acquired a fiancé, my parents urged me to drop out and go to Katherine Gibbs Secretarial School. I'll bet my real father would have told me, "Go for it. Do your best. I did." I like to think of him this way, but now he's lost in the mist of time -- an idol, some kind of Zeus looking down from the distant summit of Mt. Rainier.

My mouth blossoms with cold sores. My back aches. What in me has come from Hans Pederson, this icon of pioneer history lauded in newspaper articles and Victorian library volumes? Some of those soporific lists of his accomplishments would set people nodding at a Chamber of Commerce dinner. My mother married this old man? He was my father? He belonged in history books. Yet my mother had changed the subject whenever I asked about him. Maybe he'd had a secret criminal life. Maybe he'd been a greedy and rapacious entrepreneur, respected on the surface but rotten to the core.

Only a trip to Seattle will help me learn about this father who died so long ago. I might find some of his buildings, unless they've been razed to make way for an Interstate. Maybe I can get to know him by osmosis, by simply walking around Seattle. I decide to go in 2007, shortly after my 74th birthday, by then already five years older than he was when he had died.

Prior to my departure, I download pictures of his reputed projects from the University of Washington archives. Early photos record the bombed-out look of Seattle after the fire of 1889, jagged tree trunks rising in a sea of mud and rubble, soon to be replaced by scenes of construction everywhere.

In one photo, a mother in a straw hat, ruffled white shirtwaist blouse, and voluminous long black skirt crosses the street holding the hand of a little boy who skips beside her in black knickers and a white blouson shirt. She could have been Marie Pederson, holding Hans Jr.'s hand.

Horse-drawn carriages clip-clop beside them. Such cumbersome fashions, worn in the path of heavy construction, in the mud, the dirt, the dust, next to horses passing underneath the scaffolding. But there walk the ladies in their street-sweeping black gowns, dodging horse plops, holding wide-brimmed hats against the wind and the rain.

With a list of my father's projects in hand, I contact Seattle's Museum of History and Industry known to locals by its acronym MOHAI. Eager to take a trip into a past that I never had, I'm ready to look for my father's buildings and whatever remaining downtown Seattle sidewalks might hold his etched "signature" — his logo.

6. Sleuthing in Seattle

I join Wendy and Matt, my daughter and son-in-law, on a Pacific Northwest tour that will include two days in Seattle. We will visit museums. We decide to focus on two of my father's projects, the Seattle sidewalks and the Narada apartments on Queen Anne, where we lived when I was born. I carry a fistful of Internet photos downloaded from the University of Washington and MOHAI archives.

Soon it becomes clear that understanding Pederson's work will require more trips and further study. especially for one of his projects: the huge hydroelectric dam on the Nisqually River. I'm curious to find out more about this giant project for the city of Tacoma, on which he was the only bidder. Tacoma Public Utilities began generating electricity from this project nearly 100 years ago. The La Grande Dam, completed by Pederson in 1912 was rebuilt in 1945. Tacoma Power states: "La Grande Dam feeds water to a unique powerhouse built in 1912. Tacoma Power updated the powerhouse in 1945 by adding a 40,000-kilowatt generator to the original four 6,000-kilowatt units."

Today the Dam performs another valuable service. In the 1.7-mile-long stretch of river between LaGrande Dam and its powerhouse, Tacoma Power maintains a continuous flow of water to enhance Chinook and Coho salmon spawning habitat. The U.S. V Washington 1974 Decision affirmed the rights of several Washington tribes to harvest up to 50% of the return of salmon run within their traditional territories. Having learned of broken U.S treaties with Indian tribes over salmon fishing rights, especially on the Columbia River, it is gratifying to learn of the long reach of this Pederson project.

Otto Brask, a Seattle resident originally from Denmark, has studied Pederson's life. He describes the Tacoma project in detail:

"Construction of the hydro project to harness the Nisqually River, fed by glaciers on Mount Rainier, is said to have begun in February 1910. Building roads and railroad lines in the mountainous wilderness far from the city was only the beginning. Erecting shops, housing and dining hall for 300 workers, getting a locomotive, railroad cars, wagon loads of tools and six steam engines up to that remote site in the hills, as well as arranging purchase of cement, gravel, timber, and steel, would tax any contractor. Pederson was on top of it all. He also spent months negotiating with bankers and investors back east, as he struggled to sell the bonds to finance the construction."

Once the massive project was completed, a City of Tacoma engineer who visited the site asked Pederson, "What is your background and qualifications for this job?"

"I was a bricklayer's helper," he replied.

Wendy and I huddle under an umbrella in the morning drizzle as Matt hails a taxi in front of our hotel. "The Pioneer Building," he tells the driver in his commanding bass voice. "We're taking the underground sidewalk tour."

"I've never done that," says the 60ish driver as he eases into traffic. "I've lived in Seattle all my life, but I'd never even heard of those sidewalks until 10 years ago. You oughta go see the Ballard Bridge and the Locks too. They can change the water level 26 feet in 15 minutes to send a ship straight through those locks from Lake Washington to Puget Sound."

Maybe some other trip. We gather at a former Prohibition speakeasy next door to the Pioneer Building. After we introduce ourselves to the guide, she starts us off by saying, "Who would think that the daughter of the man who built these sidewalks would show up one hundred years later to take my tour?" We chuckle as I feel a child's pride welling up inside me.

We follow along behind her, past a parking garage, and descend a stairway into an anteroom, another former speakeasy. Taking shallow breaths to protect our lungs from air mustier than a subway station's, we listen to the guide regale us with colorful tales of old Seattle as she leads us along wood-planked "sidewalks" cleared of trash to make an aisle for the tour. I figure she'll be glad to get home and wash her fuzzy pilled sweater and her shoulder-length blond hair. She's wearing granny boots and thick wool socks -- maybe to protect herself from gnawing rats.

We creep along, inhaling shallow breaths of fetid air. Dim light shines from occasional rows of glass beads embedded in the concrete sidewalks above us that allow overhead daylight to penetrate. Arms pinned to her sides, Wendy stoops to avoid spidery webs of ancient fabric that drip from roughhewn ceiling beams. Angles open into chambers, the former first stories of sunken buildings. Rounding a corner, we edge past a grimy circular couch, its satin-tufted upholstery draped with a red chemise to evoke the bawdy days of old Seattle.

We stroll around the downtown after the tour ends, searching for my father's logo in the sidewalks. But we are too late. These sidewalks have either been replaced or are so cracked they soon will be.

We follow the taxi driver's suggestion after lunch and tour the Ballard Locks and the Lake Washington Ship Canal. Constructed in 1917 to open maritime transportation between Lake Washington and Puget Sound, the environmental cost came afterward. Two years later we learn that while the flashy contractor James A. Moore once bid on the project, Hans Pederson instead won the contract to build the Locks for the Army Corps of Engineers.

Next we ride up Queen Anne hill, Seattle's highest, to the Narada apartments on Highland Drive, our home when I was born. Mom once gave a photo of the place to my daughter Wendy when Wendy took a business trip to Seattle. Chip and I had also toured Seattle many years before Wendy's trip, but Mother never suggested that I visit my birthplace. Once in a while she'd bring my baby book off the shelf in the back of her closet and show me my infant photos; me in the arms of my Aunt Alice, or cradled by Mother's friend Dagmar. My embroidered white christening dress reaches several feet toward the ground as they hold me close on the fire escape of our fifth-floor penthouse on Highland Drive.

I grew up in New York City where I listened to immigrants kibitzing outdoors on old metal fire escapes in various accents. So, when I saw those baby photos, I figured we'd lived in a tenement, not a penthouse. I can't help wondering why Mom was so reticent. Her only statement had been, "this is where you came home to from the hospital." Since the subject made her uncomfortable, I never pursued it. In retrospect, I believe she was looking for an opening to tell me about her fear and loneliness at being in a strange city where, although she had money, she had no family support. Eventually, she might have even told me of the hostility she later faced from the family of my father's first wife. I imagine they were more than a bit surprised and dismayed that Hans remarried just months after Marie's death.

Most of all, I think she just wanted some expression of love and appreciation from me. But both of us were too prickly to cross this line. I am always touched when one of my children sends me a sentimental birthday or Mother's Day card. Yet, feeling a need to keep my distance from Mother all my life, I always sent her jokey or lighthearted cards. I never dared to show intimacy. Then when I became a mother, I realized that children take their cues from their parents. It's the parent's responsibility to set the example for loving action. I tried to show my kids how much I loved them, because I knew what it felt like to yearn for it. Even so, I wish I had shown her more love.

The Narada sits on a steep lot at the top of Highland Drive, a boulevard that circles Queen Anne hill. It's an extremely hazardous site.

The slippery clay edge once slid down 100 feet during rainstorms to settle on the boulevard below.

The city asked my father if he could stop this muddy hillside from sliding down into the middle of Queen Anne. Mud slides continue to be an ongoing threat in the Northwest. A devastating slide in the spring of 2014 covered one square mile, killed 43 people and destroyed many more lives in the town of Oso, north of Seattle.

My father went to work, determined to make the hillside of Queen Anne safe. He moved a steam pile-driving outfit from the waterfront and drove creosote piling and railroad ties onto the steep hillside, followed by concrete. Evidently he succeeded, because our building perched at the top became a coveted location. Forty years after Pederson's death, Victor White describes the building in an article he wrote for the *Frontier Times*.

"In a remarkably short period, the Narada Apartments, a beautiful brick building with five stories above West Highland Drive and three floors below street level with an unsurpassable view from every apartment was refusing tenants because of complete occupancy -- before it was completed. It had a waiting list for occupancy all through the Depression."

My father's Victoria Apartments rise next to the Narada above terraced gardens that lead to Kerry Park where today's sightseers still enjoy a panoramic view of downtown Seattle and the Space Needle. I slide a quarter into the viewfinder along the fence that marks the 100-foot drop off below the Victoria, then rotate the handle to take in the distant snow-capped view of the Olympic Mountains. The sun emerges along with a slight breeze and I imagine my father's breath over my shoulder. It feels as if he has arranged this rare day of sunshine especially for our visit.

Wendy dashes up the terraced garden path. "Mom, Mom. Quick. It's the Narada." She stops to sweep her ash-blond hair off her neck and up over her head.

A rangy man in pressed khakis holds out his hand in front of the building. "Fred Larijani. Manager. It is an honor to meet Hans Pederson's daughter." He tells me that the Narada's present owner is only the second since my father's estate sold the building. The Narada has always remained fully occupied, as sturdy as the day it was completed.

We walk up and down the steps and around the building, rubbernecking in all directions. That evening we have cocktails at Seattle's Space Needle, a visible remnant of the 1962 World's Fair. Looking down at the city from the circling observation deck, we pick out the Narada, hugging the hillside like a fort.

The next day Matt points the car northeast toward the Cascades, taking the twisting mountain roads like the stunt pilot that he is. We stop at Roslyn – the little ski town chosen as the site for Matt's favorite TV series, *Northern Exposure*. A local gift shop is stuffed with *Northern Exposure* mugs, t-shirts and hats. Wendy lingers as we leave and surreptitiously buys a hat and a mug for Matt's birthday. We move on to other restored railroad towns that dot the Cascade ski country; Cle Elum, Leavenworth, Skykomish, and Gold Bar. Marquees at each station commemorate the history of the Northern Pacific Railroad's march to the West Coast. Pleased at the chance to view such magnificent country in my lifetime, I try to imagine my father's elation as he worked his way from Wisconsin through the mountain wilderness and pictured life's possibilities ahead.

I soon learn in Victor White's article that Milwaukee Railroad workers later found a stretch of slippery mountain on the west side of the Cascades.

"It was Hans Pederson, inexperienced in railroad construction, who took the contract and made it stick. He simply said, 'This is only a few miles from Cedar River; I built the city water viaduct and know how to deal with this kind of soil.'"

Trains with a hundred miles of freight still come pounding down that slope.

Wendy and Matt fly home the next day. I take a taxi across the floating bridge to Don and Charlene's home on Mercer Island. They maintain an interest in my project since Don began my search at the King County Courthouse when he plodded through the microfiche records of both Pedersons. Entering their house, I find myself in a glass-walled aerie -- only a few feet from a lush rainforest.

I hug Charlene and Don, who still enjoys his college track-star physique. "You've settled in the wilderness," I say as Molly, their toy poodle, sniffs my shoes.

Charlene laughs, her head a circle of curls. "Yes, we like the forest primeval out here, although it can be damp." From their dining room I notice a stately tree trunk carved with totems, a local custom followed by tree surgeons as they work.

The next day, Don drops me off for an afternoon at the MOHAI to do some research. I stroll through exhibits documenting the immigrant experience with an emphasis on the growth of Seattle. Here is a pictorial history of what I have been reading for eight years. Carolyn Marr, the librarian, presents me with a photo of the James Madison School, one of Pederson's later buildings. Then she hands me Victor White's 1973 *Frontier Times article, "Seattle's Little Known Dynamo."*

Tears blur my sight when I see my father's photo under the headline. Instead of the black suited figure who appears to belong in a gold-framed ancestor portrait on the wall of some stuffy old club, a virile, handsome man with thick white hair meets my eyes with a kindly gaze. The caption under the photo reads, *Hans Pederson about 1928.* Here is a picture of half my genes. I have my father's hair and his low-slung eyebrows that practically meet my lashes. Age has brought the same droop to the outer edges of my eyelids. My father wears an expression I have often seen on the face of my son, Ben. He has a nose like mine, like my daughter Wendy, like my sons Ben and Ed; both of them self-taught contractors like their grandfather. We'd always wondered where they got their instinct to build and fix things. This photo shows neither the stiff Victorian notable in the library archives, nor the pathetic, sad and puffy-faced figure in the obituary. The strength of his character stands out in his direct gaze, the intelligent suggestion of a smile, his snowy mane. Here is the reason I have come to Seattle.

I wonder which photo is of the man my mother knew. I wonder how fast was his final decline. Mother once apologized for having no photograph of my father. "It got lost in a fire," she said. Fires were convenient. Another time Dad told me he didn't actually know Mother's age or her birthday. "The town records burned in a fire," she'd told him. Her siblings have no recollection of this fire.

Mother did once tell Ben that he looked like his grandfather. That must have been why she gave him a four-inch stack of stock certificates when he worked for a brokerage firm in 1983. After my father returned from the Klondike, he gained an interest in the Alaska Dano Mines Company and the Alaska Reindeer Company, among others.

"These belonged to your grandfather," Mother told Ben. "See if they're worth anything."

"Guess she's releasing another secret," I told him. "Look them up." Ben did, but they were worthless.

Victor White knew my father. In his article White called him:

"A remarkable citizen about whom very little has ever been heard or written. He was without formal education, social, family, business connections, or financial resources. Yet he performed feats that 'couldn't be done.' He never received publicity, never made a fortune, or sought special recognition and never belonged extensively to golf clubs, yacht clubs or fraternal orders. But he did more than any other one man to literally build Seattle … His satisfaction seemed to come from conquering difficulties and building things rather than getting rich."

His fortunes rose and fell as he gradually built up the capital to finance ever-larger projects. White compares him to Howard Hughes; both of them were "genius-type" men." Both always seemed to win. Both gambled -- Hughes on anything, Pederson on construction. Hughes' name was often associated with women. Pederson's never was. Although Hughes always had money and Pederson sometimes did, neither one carried cash. Sorensen, one of Pederson's foremen, (whose first name was not recorded once said, "Hans has never carried any money. He would often visit a job around lunchtime and borrow a quarter from me for a sandwich and a cup of coffee."

He radiated energy. A March 27, 1931 Christian Science Monitor article states that "his friends declare that the making of money was not his main object: instead, *"The construction of something worthwhile in buildings."* One time a tenant in his Fionia apartments complained that she needed an easy chair. He had one in the basement of the Brewer, several blocks away. When someone suggested a truck, he said, "No, I can go get it and carry it over here. I am strong enough to do that." Later that day, the white-haired man in his early sixties returned, carrying an overstuffed chair.

Hans never owned a car. He hitched rides or took streetcars wherever he went. So much for mother's assertion that my father had died driving to work, blinded by the angle of the early morning sun.

I keep White's photo close beside me for the rest of the day. That night I weep for the father I never knew. If only I could have received his love, his counsel and guidance. If only he could have enjoyed his only child for more than twenty-eight days.

I awake the next morning with a migraine. Don has planned a downtown excursion to search for my father's buildings. He paces the kitchen under the watchful eye of Molly, their poodle, while I sip weak tea and nibble toast. We drag out of the house shortly before noon.

Downtown Seattle bears little resemblance to the early twentieth century University of Washington photos. Wide streets and grassy

95

squares surrounded by Model T cars have given way to a hodgepodge of buildings and architectural styles. The red brick face of the Arctic Club at Third and Cherry has been whitewashed. Looking up, I notice a row of walrus heads; tusks curving inwards like spears, surrounding the third floor exterior. A sign at the entrance announces a remodeling project. Peering through the windows under the overhanging façade with a trey ceiling, we observe stacks of lumber and carpenters' tool aprons, but not a worker in sight at lunch hour.

I trudge half a block along the sidewalk behind Don until we reach the King County Courthouse. Several articles credit my father not only with the original two-story courthouse, but also with the six-story addition.

"Look!" Don stops abruptly. He points to the bronze plaque embedded in the face of the building

KING COUNTY COURTHOUSE
COMPLETED 1930

COUNTY COMMISSIONERS
DON EVANS • CHAIRMAN
WM. BROWN
WILMER B. BRINTON

ARCHITECTS
HENRY BITTMAN
JOHN L. MCCAULEY

CONTRACTOR
HANS PEDERSON

King County Courthouse at City Hall Square, Seattle WA. Printed by permission from UW Library archives.

At last. The physical proof of my father's work. Again I feel the pull of history, the pride of kinship. The King County Courthouse that my father built holds the Pedersons' wills, the wills found by Don that enabled me to begin my quest.

I leave Seattle with a sense of my father. I have seen his work. At home, I frame his handsome photo and hang it on my bedroom wall. Those who wrote of him ascribed his success to hard work and canny bidding. Some hinted that he buried his grief over the death of his adopted son in his work. But what about his Danish wife, Marie Madsen? What about his second wife, my mother?

Carolyn Marr, the MOHAI librarian, steers me to one more source. An oral history from *New Land New Lives, Scandinavian Immigrants to the Pacific Northwest*, assembled from tapes compiled by Janet E. Rasmussen.

One tape features the voice of Laura Madsen Foss, who came to Seattle at the age of 15 to help her aunt, Marie Madsen Pederson, who bought her ticket. Laura speaks of her Uncle Hans only once. "He came running to the station to meet my train. He had white hair and never wore a hat." This is her only mention of him, although she praises others in her life: Dad, Granddad, brothers, sisters, minister, husband, friends. She has good things to say about everyone except her crabby and demanding Aunt Marie. According to Laura, Marie was mean. She separated Laura from her cousin, her traveling companion from Denmark. She made Laura memorize a grocery list, then sent her out alone to the meat market before Laura learned to speak English. She got lost. She couldn't remember what to buy. Fortunately, the butcher knew Marie and helped Laura with the order. Marie expected 15-year-old Laura to work and pay her own way. She allowed her to attend the Danish school in Solvang, California, where she had to earn her room and board. When Laura's many chores left her no time to study, the principal absolved her of some duties. Still, Marie told Laura she must reimburse the principal for her room and board.

Laura implied that Hans was rarely home. Marie was diabetic. Laura helped her give dinner parties for their friends, but these elderly guests bored her. Laura enjoyed the Lutheran youth group at the Danish Church, generously funded by the Pedersons. She met her husband there and later appreciated the nice wedding the Pedersons gave her in their Narada penthouse apartment at the top of Queen Anne. She notes that her rich uncle owned the whole complex, but the guests at the reception were all old people. It appears that the Pedersons, known for their hard work and frugality, expected more of Laura. Their experience as immigrants had taught them that nobody would do it for them. Only the bold and nimble overcame the challenges of the rigorous West.

In trying to decipher my father's life, I've found a smattering of odds and ends. There is still so much I don't know. It has been said that people who investigate their roots are not those who had a close or comfortable relationship with their parents. Their quest is a search for understanding -- for the loss or feeling of abandonment that remains with them no matter how comfortable their physical existence.

One time I said to Mother, "Please tell me something about my father. My children and I need to learn about our heritage, about our genes. We need to be something besides the stepfamily."

She gave her engagement ring from Hans Pederson to my son, Jeff, his eldest grandson. She gave my father's stock certificates to my son, Ben. She gave a photo of the Narada apartments to my daughter Wendy on her first trip to Seattle. My half-sister, Cookie, got hold of my father's estate settlement records, as well as my adoption certificate. Cookie never showed me either one of them until long after Mother died. Odd that Mother never gave anything directly to me to then pass down to my children. She simply skipped over me, but I'm grateful that she was thoughtful with my children.

When I finally got the nerve to ask my mother what my father was like, I so hoped she would share with me. I can't explain why I was so afraid to ask. She replied in an aggrieved tone, "He built some buildings. He was a very nice man. Everybody liked him." It was as if she resented my curiosity.

Why?

PART II
MY LIFE 1933-1960

7. Expatriate Memories

When my father died in Seattle a month after my birth, he left Mother not only with me, but also with a complex legal mess. She soon learned of extensive claims on her husband's enterprises -- unpaid mortgages, taxes, insurance, and maintenance on his vast properties. He hadn't paid his bills because his debtors hadn't paid him. Whatever Mother knew about his first wife, Marie, was probably not connected with her financial interests. It turned out that not only had she shared Pederson's home for forty-two years, she had also shared the ownership of his business.

Mother brought her youngest sister, Alice, from Canada to care for me while she figured out how to move on with her life during the time that her lawyers were settling her husband's estate. She did not lack for suitors. She once told me that she broke her engagement to Elmer, a scientist who later helped develop the atom bomb, after she met my stepdad, Everett, on a cruise, because she thought she would have a more interesting life with Everett. She used to call Dad 'Ever,' a nickname that reflected her hope for stability and security. She married him when I was two and a half.

I found several packets of Dad's letters to Mother on the back shelf of a closet when I cleared out the Maine cottage before the 2004 remodeling. Hesitating, knowing I was a voyeur, I opened them and began to follow my parents' early hopes and dreams for their life together. Their love was urgent, ardent, fueled by their frequent separations. Reading these letters brought not only a flood of memories, but also a greater understanding of events that had taken place during my childhood.

————

Forty-six-year old Dad, eighteen years Mother's senior, traveled the Orient as Far Eastern Manager for STANCO, a Standard Oil subsidiary. STANCO sold FLIT; a powerful insecticide that prevented many cases of malaria.

Dad had already spent fourteen years in the Far East as part of an army of expatriate businessmen by the time he met Mother. Their work was limited mostly to travel between coastal and Yangtze River ports where westerners were permitted to live and trade according to treaties established between the Peking (Beijing) government and foreign countries. While some foreigners, mostly missionaries, ventured inland, travel was primitive and uncertain away from the protection of the treaty ports.

American corporations treated their workers well for taking these risks. During the 1930s, the solid benefits that went with corporate jobs saved international businessmen from the struggles of U.S. workers. Expat families lived in compounds with numerous servants. They played golf and tennis and dined at clubs. They enjoyed bridge, booze, and dancing. After Mother's brief marriage to a man old enough to be her grandfather, she had found a somewhat younger man who would come into her life to serve as a refuge of strength and stability.

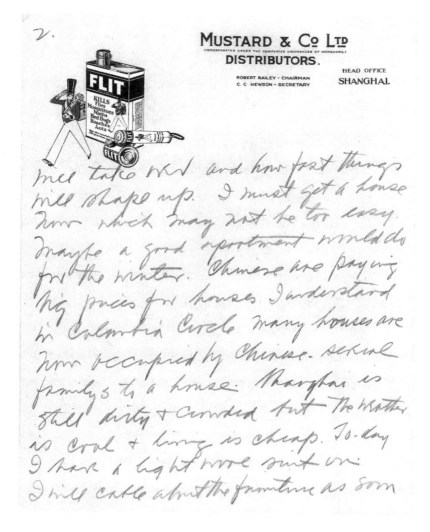

As I read their letters I go back in time to the memory of them going away to get married.

My Auntie Alice is taking care of me. We go to the ship. Mommy is going away with my new Daddy to get married then Mommy will come home. She kisses me. Her hat is big on her face. She smells powdery like when I have a bath. I love how she always dries me with the big towel, and then she sings to me and rubs powder on me. I hug her.

Mommy puts me down. My new Daddy picks me up. He is big. His eyes are furry on top. He kisses me and then he puts me down. He takes Mommy's hand and they walk away from me.

"There they are. They're going up the gangplank," Auntie Alice says.

They wave. The ship is so big I can't see it all. They throw things.

"Look! Paper streamers," Auntie Alice says. "Let's try and catch them." But we can't. They fall in the water.

"They're leaving now, let's wave," Auntie Alice says.

The ship makes a big noise. I push my face hard with my hands.

"Don't cry. They'll be back soon. You will have a Mommy and a Daddy."

The ship gets small. It goes away. Auntie Alice is comfy and soft.

They married in Singapore in January 1936. They had only a week's honeymoon in Bombay (Mumbai) before Mother set off on a return trip to the States via an Italian ship. Dad was bereft without her.

"Dear Doris,

This is my first letter and I'm so lost without you, Darling that I can't think what to say. I miss you so much, it's terrible. We had a brief departure on the ship, there was little time. I saw you leave the rail and go inside to your cabin. Well, you had to go sometime and it was sure to be difficult. I have thought of you all the time since you left and my face has not had any smiles. Darling, I wonder what I am doing being without you. I suppose India could be bearable if you were here, but as it is, it's the same dreary place it has always been. You should be a happy girl going home to your baby, Darling, and I know you won't be able to get there quick enough. You know how much I love you and want you; Darling, and I'll only be waiting until we can be together again."

———

I remember that time so vividly.

Mommy is coming home. Auntie Alice told Mommy's friend, Dagmar that my daddy said to watch out for those crazy wop soldiers of Il Duce. Mommy's New York postcard with big buildings says, "I'm a Standard Oil lady now, so I stopped at STANCO. It was okay." Now she's on the train to Seattle to see me. Then we'll go to China.

———

STANCO was only okay? On meeting Mother, STANCO executives may have deduced that Dad's marriage was about to bring an end to the loyal company man who for years had been willing to go anywhere and endure any hardship for the sake of the company.

Mother probably realized that her youth, beauty, and wealth would threaten the status quo. Perhaps there was a hint that Dad was not quite the powerful executive she thought she had married.

His letters continued their near-daily declarations of love.

"I am only waiting for the days to pass until we are together again and not until then can I again enjoy the happiness I have when I'm with you. I sometimes wonder if anyone had to separate so soon after marriage as we did and then go in opposite directions around the world. Such a trying experience to have to go through."

———

"Oh Doris, I'm so happy for you," Auntie Alice says when Mommy gets home.

"Yes." Mommy folds Daddy's letter. "Pretty soon we'll all be together. We'll be a real family."

Auntie Alice comes with us when we go on the ship to China. She takes care of me in our big Shanghai house. It's hot and I get sticky when she holds me in her lap. After a while she goes away on a ship back to Seattle.

I have fun with Mommy. We play with my dolls. She goes out to lunch and bridge when I have my nap. When Daddy is home they eat and go dancing at the Columbia Club or the French Club. I stay home with Amah.

———

Dad traveled constantly to Manila, Saigon, and Singapore. Business was good. He always seemed to write in haste to catch the mail boat or clipper. Depending on the connections, letters could take months. What a frustrating life for him.

"I have missed you so much, Darling, that I don't know how I am going to stand it until April. It's terrible! Do you think you want to come to Europe or wait and meet me in New York? My travel plans change but my times in Java, Singapore, and India should be about the same. I'm wondering when I'll ever hear from you. I expect to leave Manila, Dec. 9th, arrive Saigon the 12th and arrive Singapore about Dec. 22. There are few boats to French Indochina [Vietnam] and it is difficult to arrange connections.

Does Paula ever talk about me? I miss her so much. Give her a kiss for me and tell her to be a good girl and not to forget her daddy."

He constantly exhorted me to be a good girl. As for Mother, how self-sufficient and adaptable she was! While many American wives hated the constant shifts in strange cultures, Mother thrived on her new experiences. She had her own income from the uncontested part of Hans Pederson's estate, as well as a successful husband, household servants, and luxurious travel with shipboard babysitters. A natural athlete, she soon mastered golf, a game she played into her eighties. Wherever she went, Dad arranged companionship for her with friends and associates who were happy to entertain his beautiful young bride.

Dad assured her that he could provide for her. He bought gold shares, annuities, and made Mother the beneficiary of his insurance policies. His will was in safekeeping at the STANCO office in New

York. He sent her a record of his holdings and apologized several times that he couldn't mail her a Christmas present. He generally dashed off letters in a rush to get them aboard the next ship, and he constantly revised his travel plans so he could see us.

————

More memories reveal themselves to me as I read Dad's letters.

Pretty soon it's my new Daddy's home leave. We get on another ship and go to Seattle where I used to be a baby. Mommy goes to her lawyers. She comes home all mad. Then we drive to New York in a car for a very long time. One day we go to Yellowstone Park.

They want to see Old Faithful geyser but it's too far for me to walk.

"Stay in the car," Mommy says. She gives me a chocolate bar. "And whatever you do, keep the window closed because a bear might come."

I stand on the back seat and watch them go. I don't cry. There's no grass where they walk. Yellowstone Park is not like Seattle. It's not like Shanghai. The car gets hot, so I scrunch down on my legs and they get sticky. I take the paper off the chocolate bar. It starts to melt, so I lick my fingers. I turn the handle to open the window a little hoping to cool down.

I look up. I see a black bear.

He's so big! He sniffs at me with his big nose. Maybe he's hungry. I turn the window handle some more. I drop out chocolate for him. He eats it off the ground and goes away. I laugh. He is so funny.

But if I tell Mommy, she will yell and say I'm not a good girl. They left me by myself while they go on their secret walk to their secret place. Now I have a secret too.

I recall after home leave we go back to Honolulu on another ship. I remember standing high up on the deck, looking over the railing.

We throw streamers like a rainbow. Daddy takes pictures. The ship honks a big long noise and we leave. It's like when Mommy and Daddy got married and I stayed with Auntie Alice, but Auntie Alice isn't here. Who will they leave me with now? I bite my hand. I don't like these ships. But I'm happy this time they are taking me with them.

The rugs are deep. Some rugs are on the wall. I don't make noise when we walk in the big rooms with pictures on the ceiling. Mommy and Daddy eat at the Captain's table. I eat in the children's dining room. At our tea party we have little cakes with swirly icing. The lady in the white dress takes care of me. She gives me baths in the salt water from the ocean that comes into the tub. She brushes my teeth and helps me put on my pajamas when Mommy and Daddy are dancing. She turns out the light. I look out the porthole at the moon. I hug my bear and I go to sleep.

The next day I have to go to the bathroom. The ship is rocking. I hold the toilet seat with both hands so I won't fall in. I'm too high up. The ship goes sideways. The door opens and bangs against the wall. Daddy looks around the corner. He takes my picture with his camera. He laughs. He laughs again and goes away. He pulls the door closed.

I cry. Why did he take that mean picture? You're supposed to knock if the door is closed. My daddy said this when I saw him in the bedroom in his BVD underwear. You're supposed to wait until the person says, "come in." But my daddy pushed that door open. He took my picture on the potty and then went out again. Laughing! He always tells me to be a good girl. Is he a good daddy?

Dad's potty photo of me turned out to be my parents' favorite. Using it as a model, an artist created a pastel drawing of my head. A blond Dutch bob frames my face; my blue eyes, round with surprise, look up from my button nose and kewpie-doll mouth. My parents hung the drawing between the carved teakwood headboards of their twin beds. Still, even though the artist sweetened my expression of despair into one of cherubic surprise, for the rest of my life I've felt betrayed whenever I look at that drawing.

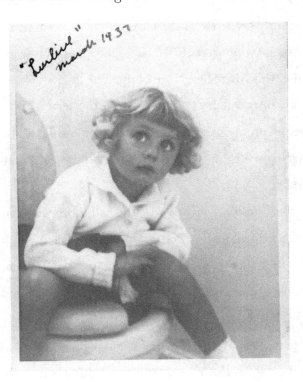

The same artist did a second pastel from another photo of me two years later. My parents chose that artist, because at a New Year's Eve party, he noticed Mother seated on the arm of a couch and asked if he could sketch her. In the drawing she reigns regal and haughty, her gaze somewhere in the distance, somehow unapproachable in her sapphire blue gown with spaghetti straps. That portrait always hung in the living room until Cookie moved it to her house just before I came to Greensboro for her daughter's wedding. When Mother asked which of us would get the portrait, I said "Cookie," and hastened to add, "Because I have the other two you had done of me."

"Two!" Cookie headed for the basement in a snit. "They never had one done of me." Cookie was only one-year old when the pastels of me were done, and I was five. I guess we both feel slighted in one way or another.

––––––––

The bill for Mother's two-week maternity stay at Honolulu's Kapiolani Hospital was $103.28 for Cookie's 1937 birth. Dad left for Shanghai shortly afterwards. He was not prepared for conditions as he approached the city early in 1938 on the *Empress of Japan*. Like many westerners, he preferred the clean, efficient, and orderly Japanese to the seemingly chaotic Chinese. The Japanese appeared to be an American ally. The *Empress of Japan*, a first class ocean liner, did not censor the mails. As tensions mounted in Europe, Americans avoided European ships.

113

In July 1937, the Japanese invaded Peking (Beijing), and took control of the Marco Polo Bridge. They later bombed Shanghai in the "Bloody Saturday" bombing memorialized in J.G. Ballard's book, *Empire of the Sun*, later made into the Stephen Spielberg film. The Japanese controlled most of Shanghai, with the exception of the French Concession, by the time Dad arrived in Shanghai. The foreign settlement became a temporary island of safety for Chinese refugees who poured into "Frenchtown," seeking safety, pushing carts overflowing with their worldly possessions.

———

Dad's letters note the changes.

"It takes a few days to come to a definite opinion. I have met lots of people and have been all over the ruins of Chapei. Sunday I went out to Hongkew Road to the airport. Destruction everywhere and few people around, all very depressing. I have talked to nobody who is optimistic about the future of China or Shanghai. It is the belief that the war will last another year or more. The only business here now is that in the [foreign] settlements which are crowded with refugees. Dirty beggars are a nuisance. Dead bodies in the streets. Japanese soldiers control the Garden Bridge and you have to pass them to go to the Broadway Mansions. No shops have opened on the Hongkew side of the Garden Bridge. Almost no shipping in the river except Japanese boats. No cargo comes from the interior.

All houses and apartments in Frenchtown are full as it's the safest place. The Columbia Club and French Club are as usual. It is a funny thing, business is dead and the outlook bad, but still the clubs, theatres and night joints are chock full. Except for seeing an occasional truck of Japanese soldiers, you wouldn't know there is a war. But the streets are crowded with Chinese, the paper said 50,000 came today from the country. It's impossible to get away from them. The well-to-do Chinese have all left and only the scum remain in Shanghai.

Mustard, [Dad's FLIT distributor] has cut their staff and closed branch offices. They have moved next door to a fourth-floor suite. Now all they have left is Shanghai and Hong Kong. The other territories require so little time that it is not worthwhile for the Company to keep me out here. It looks like they will either send me to South Africa or take me back to New York. I would prefer the latter, even if they transfer me to another department of the Company. I want you to live anywhere I am, Honey, but Shanghai business is dead and there is likely to be so much sickness with so many dead bodies around and so many filthy refugees in the city.

I think China and Japan will be fighting for years. Whoever wins the war, business will be bad for the foreigner. I think China is finished as far as foreigners are concerned and I am anxious to get established somewhere else as soon as possible."

––––––––

He was right about business, but wrong about World War II. China would become America's ally, Japan, her enemy.

While Dad bemoaned the decline of China for foreign businessmen, dedicated western doctors and missionaries remained in

Shanghai to help combat the cholera and smallpox brought to the International Settlement by more than a million Chinese refugees. The epidemic spread rapidly due to the impossibility of sanitary disposal of waste and dead bodies.

————

Daddy is in Shanghai. He can't come see us in Honolulu, so we're moving to Manila. Daddy wants Mommy to bring our maid, Honako, on the ship with us. Mommy told her friend that she's supposed to buy Honako a one-way ticket and leave her in Kobe, Japan. Honako is supposed to stay on the lower deck because she is Japanese, but the purser thinks she can stay with us if we book two staterooms. I hope Cookie stays in Honako's stateroom so I can stay with Mommy. But Honako doesn't want to leave Honolulu, so we go by ourselves."

You have to get used to walking around on the ship. I even keep my arms out to the side. We lean back and forth so we won't slide into the wall when the ship rolls on the ocean. The tables in the dining room have little fences around them. Then, if the ship goes rolling, the dishes won't crash to the floor.

I am four and a half, so I sleep on the top bunk. Cookie sleeps with Mommy on the bottom bunk. One day Mommy brings Cookie up to the top bunk to play with me. Cookie is five months old. She knows how to roll over.

The ship hits rough water. It jerks. Cookie falls off the top bunk. She hits the rug. She screams. I cry. Mommy yells at me. I try to hide in the corner under the ceiling. Mommy won't stop yelling, yelling, yelling about what a stupid fool I am. Mommy says Cookie might die, because I didn't watch her. I scrunch against the wall under the ceiling and cry. Mommy yells and screams for a long time.

I didn't mean to hurt my baby sister. Mommy never yells at me when Daddy is here. I tell Mommy that now Daddy will hate me too. She stops yelling and says she won't tell Daddy about this bad thing that I did, because Daddy loves us all so much. She reads me his letter.

"I will be so glad to see you and Paula and Cookie. I think so much of my girls and am so thrilled with our baby. It gives me a feeling I never experienced before. I love you so much and I am so proud of you and happy to be married to you that I simply cannot tell you what it means to me. Never in my life have I felt so attached and a part of anyone as I do with you. I hope the days pass quickly until you arrive."

With Shanghai business declining due to the Japanese occupation, Dad spent his days interviewing applicants to work as FLIT agents for Mustard, his distributor. The project kept him so busy that he thought of bringing us back to Shanghai. Back and forth they went evaluating the climate; Shanghai was too hot in the summer, Manila too hot in the spring. What would be best for the children? It was a toss-up where we should live. In the meantime, he went with friends to the French Club and bowled two or three times a week at the Columbia Club. While he continued to search for a house or apartment in Shanghai, he wrote that housing was so tight in Columbia Circle that several Chinese families occupied each house. With their extensive gardens, fountains, and circular drives, these homes offered ample space for more than one family, especially for desperate Chinese refugees who did not require eight to twelve servants.

Dad's travels and Mother's independence combined to keep him off balance. His letters assured her that he would reimburse her for her expenses, but transferring funds generally took two months, just as letters did. A September 1938 letter from Shanghai began, *"I called you yesterday as I 'collapsed' when I did not get any mail from you on the Japan. Did you hurt your wrist bowling?"*

A bunch of Mother's letters finally arrived on another ship. I had not been well, so she thought it best that we stay in Manila. Dad replied, "Well, I guess it's settled we stay in Manila for the winter. I got your last cable, but there is no 'love' in it. Are you economizing?" He wrote "A-1" when her letters arrived. He told Mother she must get a cook.

He was pleased at the progress of Hans Pederson's settlement.

"I am glad you had a good letter from Padden and that things look good. I know it is exasperating when there is no news and it takes a lot of patience sometimes. Of course I hope you will be a 'millionairess' one day. It would be most becoming to you. I guess you can be sure it will all be settled by the time you go home."

It wasn't settled until 1941, four years later. By that time Pederson's creditors, Marie's relatives, and the attorneys had picked at it for eight long years through the ongoing Depression. The settlement never provided Mother with the life she felt she deserved. Her anger at the final tally seeped through her like a slow poison for the rest of her days, even though her holdings supplemented Dad's salary and provided us with luxuries.

At first, Dad's oblique suggestions and criticisms might have been interpreted as compliments. He praised Mother constantly, telling her what a wonderful wife and mother she was, how brilliant and talented Cookie and I were, thanks to her. But he also mentioned the Dale Carnegie bestseller, *How to Win Friends and Influence People.* Rather than tell people what was wrong with them, Carnegie wrote, it was more productive to motivate them with praise. Dad had begun to notice the cracks in Mother's vaunted charm. Unfortunately, she never got the message. All through my childhood, she'd invariably follow her blasts at me with the comment, "I'm only telling you what's wrong with you for your own good, so you can improve yourself." I learned to tune out the hurt and retreat into silence. Listening to Mother scold Daddy or Cookie was equally disturbing. Since Mother was the center of our worlds, it seemed disloyal to question her opinions. Instead, through the years we simply stopped communicating.

Dad's letters gradually evolved into itineraries -- or rather, listings of his frustration at not settling anywhere long enough to bring us together. His beautiful, rich, young wife was spending her days with little children in expat communities filled with traveling men. Wives without husbands had limited social opportunities. In spite of Mother's good care of us and her life of leisure, she must have felt isolated and bored at times. Dad began to advise her on our care.

"I would not leave either Paula or the baby too much to the servants. They are both unusually good children and worth all the time

119

and attention you give them. Children like them are hard to find so you'll have to give them part of the attention I give them when I am home."

————

I have an amah again when we get to Manila. Costanza. Except she's a maid too. She is beautiful. She wears a regular dress with flowers instead of a blue nightgown all the way to the floor. She doesn't wear a robe with an obi sash like Honako did in Honolulu. For my birthday, I get Dionne quintuplet dolls, dressed all the same. We use FLIT from Daddy's Mustard business and we have a big fence around our yard. Pink bougainvillea flowers climb over the top like they want to come visit us.

Mommy and Daddy play golf. They each have two caddies. One caddy carries the bag. The other one gets the ball if they hit it over the wall. At the green, a caddy pokes the cup with a golf club to see if there is a cobra inside. Then he gets the ball out of the cup. Daddy plays tennis too. He has four ball boys. Each boy stands in a different corner of the tennis court so he can pick up the ball. When Mommy rides horses she wears funny pants and special boots. They bowl too. They're always going somewhere.

Francisco is our houseboy. I have fun when he waxes the floor. He walks on coconut halves on top of cloths so he can hold on with his toes. I grab his shirt, and he pulls me along for a ride.

When Daddy comes home for Christmas, we go out in the back yard. Cookie has learned to walk. Daddy is so proud. Mommy is excited. She throws her hands in the air. I take off my shoes and socks. They always wear shoes and socks. Daddy holds his socks up with garters. I run in the grass barefoot. The grass isn't soft, but it's not hard like a brush. It feels good to have no shoes. Daddy is so proud Cookie can walk. I dance around in my bare feet. There are no cobras or centipedes today.

Our maid Costanza screams one night after Daddy goes. The police come. We stay upstairs and Mommy holds me tight. Costanza's boyfriend has a knife, but he can't get in, because the windows have bars. When Daddy gets home, he tells Mommy the Filipinos are terrible people.

Costanza and Francisco are not terrible. They sing to me and play with me. I'm worried I will go to jail like Costanza's boyfriend. I took a candy bar from the store. Mommy heard the crinkly paper when I took it off. She asked me where I got the candy.

"I took it from the store."

"No! You stole it. You didn't pay for it. The police will come get you. They will take you to jail."

I run and hide under my bed. Mommy doesn't come get me. She doesn't care.

I learn to skip in Kindergarten. I'm the last one in the class to learn. Everyone sits on the floor and claps while I skip around the circle. So maybe I won't go to jail.

———

Now we live in Shanghai again. Daddy takes pictures at my birthday party. Mommy tells me my friends are German, English, Danish, and French-Italian. I don't know their names. It is hot, so I wear a hat. Daddy takes a picture of our servants. Boy, Cook, Coolie, Amah, Wash Amah. The chauffeur drives us in Daddy's big car. Amah sews red slippers with flowers on them for her small, small feet. They stick out sideways when she walks. I don't run away, because she can't catch me.

1939-Shanghai - Cookie (age 2) with Amah. Paula (age 6) Doris (age 32). We ride in rickshas to avoid floodwaters at Grosvenor House, our apartment building in the International Settlement.

In Shanghai, we live on the sixth floor of Grosvenor House, a big curvy building. Everything looks small out the window. Daddy goes to his office on the Bund at the big Jardine Matheson building and near the Cathay Hotel with the pointed roof. There is a big clock on top of the Customs House like Big Ben in London. Daddy says I can learn to tell time there. He takes trips all the time so FLIT can kill bugs. Daddy says we're lucky, because our apartment has screens. The beds have mosquito nets so bad bugs can't come in and bite us.

I'm learning to play our Moutriette piano. I don't go to the kitchen because Cook is there. Only "Boy" goes into the kitchen so he can bring us food to the dining room. They both wear long nightgowns like Amah's. Mommy tells people the funny story about Cook. He scrubbed the beans with a toothbrush. When he did it again, Mommy said, "No, I told you not to do that," but Cook said it was okay, because he used his own toothbrush. Everyone laughs at this story.

The grownups tell about the funny things the servants do. You have to look out for squeeze. That's when they buy too much food and take some home to their families. Daddy says you have to watch them or they'll steal. He says they're all like children. Mommy says it's typical of the masses. I'm glad they want to take care of their children. They might be hungry since they're all so poor.

Cookie is two now. We have our amah whose stomach sticks out in the middle of her long nightgown. Her gold tooth sparkles when she opens her mouth to smile or chatter in Chinese. Her hair is yanked to the back of her head in a curvy bunch. The top of her head looks bald. Mommy says that is the style for amahs.

Daddy takes Mommy to the tailor to make special clothes for her so she will always look pretty. Mommy has a beautiful evening dress. It is soft black velvet with white lacy flowers partway to the top. Daddy told the tailor to make it for her so she can wear it to parties at the French Club. They dance on the roof. They play bridge too.

One day Mommy has some ladies come to eat lunch and play bridge. While they eat lunch in the dining room, Boy makes three small tables and puts chairs around the tables -- four chairs for each table. Amah brings in a pile of table covers, table cloths and napkins. The colors are all mixed up, pink ones and blue ones and green ones.

"Can I help?" I ask.

"Small Misses make color," Amah says.

First I put down the table covers with gold edges. Each cover has a same color tablecloth to match.

"No wrinkle," Amah opens the tablecloths and holds them up.

Bamboo bushes are sewn all over the green tablecloth. Pagodas are on the blue one. The pink one has high mountains where you could fall off the edge. They are like beautiful pictures.

Amah puts the covers and cloths on the tables. I set down the right-colored napkins to match. Then Amah takes me to the hall to wait, because I watched Cook make live-bird cake in the kitchen. It looks like a sugar castle.

The ladies sit down at the little tables, and Cook brings the cake. He tells Mommy where to cut it and when she does, a real live bird jumps out and flies around. All the ladies laugh and scream. The live bird poops in a lady's hair. I laugh and Cook laughs, but the lady is not happy.

"Oh no, I just had a shampoo and finger wave," she says. She looks mad. Mommy tells Amah to bring some shampoo and towels to the bathroom for her.

Cook catches the bird by a string around its neck and brings it back to the kitchen. None of the ladies eat the live bird cake. I wonder if the bird pooped in the cake, so I don't eat it either.

Daddy works for STANCO. He doesn't work for Standard Oil anymore, so I don't go to the Shanghai American School with the Standard Oil kids. The missionary kids live at that school, because their parents are in the interior. Instead, I go to first grade at St. Jean d'Arc, in the French Concession. The nuns wear long black dresses and we are supposed to speak French, which I don't know. One day they make me stand in the corner. There's a dollhouse there, so I scoot down and play with the little furniture. Then they let me go back to class. I don't like it here, because I don't speak French.

Chinese men bring Mommy's new furniture. They are teakwood with carved flowers on the beds and mirrors and bureaus. Even the chairs and tables are carved. Daddy still has his rosewood coffee table and rosewood ancestor chairs. They are not comfortable for sitting. The silver cigarette box and silver ashtrays with dragons crawling around are on Daddy's coffee table. Boy always shines them.

One day Mommy yells too much. She yells, "How I sacrifice for you." I pack up Cookie's koala bear and my Dionne quintuplets, and we run away on the elevator to the second floor to the Cohens from Germany. I ring the bell and they invite us in. Mr. Cohen calls Mommy on the telephone. Mrs. Cohen makes tea with lots of milk and sugar and gives it to us in her little Meissen cups and saucers. She brings us cookies and I see she has wrinkly skin on her hands. Her face, too. Then fat Mr. Cohen takes us upstairs on the elevator and my mama gives us hugs and kisses. I wonder if she's sorry we ran away.

Mommy buys the things the Germans bring in their suitcases. She bought some little demitasse cups and saucers all decorated with flowers and leaves. Each one has a tiny silver spoon in the saucer. The spoons are pointy with flowers on the handles -- lilies of the valley, Mommy says. The spoons didn't come from the Germans, Mommy says they belonged to my father. When I show them to Daddy, he laughs and says, "I'm your Daddy, but those aren't my spoons." He puts his newspaper up to his face. It makes me feel like I did a bad thing.

Boy shines the spoons when he polishes the silver bowls and the cocktail shaker with bamboo. The shaker has a shot glass on the top for Daddy's whiskey water or his gimlet.

8. Growing Pains

Pretty soon we're evacuated, which means we have to leave Shanghai. We get on two more ships. The first one goes to Vancouver, B.C., then we get on another one and go all the way back to Honolulu. I'm seven now and I'm in the second grade. We stay in the Halekulani Hotel on Waikiki Beach while we look for a house. A lot goes on at Waikiki. There are surfers that stand right up on the surfboard and ride to the beach on the waves. They never fall off! We go swimming in the waves at one place, but the surfers go somewhere else. After we find a house, I take two buses to school all by myself. The first goes down Kahala Avenue past Diamond Head, the big volcano that sticks out on the beach. Then I transfer to the bus for Punahou School. I get to go barefoot, because you don't have to wear shoes until seventh grade in Hawaii.

We live on Aukai. Street. My best friend, Lee Lee, lives on Kahala Avenue. She has a huge kiawe tree in her yard. We sit in the shade, but we have to be careful or we'll step on thorns. They hurt, but we just yank them out. Sometimes we play records in Lee Lee's house.

You don't have to lift the needle and change the record every three minutes, because they have this brand new machine. You put a whole stack of records on and they each drop down one at a time to play. When they're all done, the machine picks up the whole pile and turns them over and plays the other side. I lie back on Lee Lee's flowered couch and listen, dangling my feet over the ends, because we're not supposed to put our dirty feet on the couch.

I take hula lessons with Mommy. Her grass skirt is green like her bra with pretend leaves. Her leis and her wrist and ankle flowers are made of gold paper -- crinkly. My hula skirt and bra and flowers are pinky-purple. The flowers look real. We both have feather gourds and bamboo sticks to use when we dance. Our lessons are in a big room with a black floor. Out the window, bougainvillea flowers look like a waterfall. Soon I go to the children's' class to learn more hula.

We have a recital and Daddy comes to watch. The other girls are smiling in Daddy's pictures. Mommy told me to smile too, but I forgot when I bowed at the end. I'm not any good. My skirt droops under my belly button and I'm holding my hands wrong. Mommy tells me I'm lucky to learn the hula and go to the beach. She says I'm lucky she buys me pretty clothes.

"You're a little doll," she says.

I feel like a doll because, I always have to get dressed up like my Dionne quintuplet dolls.

"Someone worked very hard to make your beautiful hand-smocked dresses," Mommy says. She teaches me how to curtsy when I meet people.

I read a lot. I've read most of the Nancy Drew mysteries and the Bobbsey Twins. There are 72 books about the Bobbsey Twins and I want to read all of them. When Mommy goes out and leaves me with Cookie, I have to remember not to read, because Cookie is three and you never know what she's going to do, so I must watch her closely. One day she swallows a penny. I call Lee Lee's father -- he's a doctor who helps the mothers having babies.

"I have to speak to Dr. Spencer," I tell the lady who answers the phone. "Cookie swallowed a penny."

"Stay right there and I'll tell him," she says.

Dr. Spencer tells her I should feed Cookie some bread and milk. I don't tell Mommy, because I'm afraid she might yell at me and whip me with her belt. We have fun with Mommy though. We go to the beach, rub on baby oil and get sunburns. They hurt, but then they peel, and we get new skin.

Now I am so scared. One day last summer, Mommy told me that Daddy is not really my daddy. No. He's not. My real daddy died when I was a baby. But now Daddy is my daddy because Mommy married him. He's Cookie's real daddy. She's really his little girl, but I'm not. He loves me just the same though, because I'm so pretty and I'm such a good little girl. He holds me on his lap and tells me the poem about "The Wreck of the Hesperus" by Longfellow:

"It was the schooner Hesperus

That sailed the wintery sea;

And the skipper had taken his little daughter,

To bear him company.

Blue were her eyes as the fairy flax,

Her cheeks like the dawn of day… "

Mommy said a car ran over my real daddy and we were poor until she married this daddy. She sounded all mad when she told me. I don't dare ask any more about it, since it was such a bad thing. I try to help her, because maybe it was my fault. I have to be better.

That was last summer. Now it's almost Christmas and I'm crying in the back yard behind the palm tree. There is no Santa Claus. I heard Daddy whisper, "Do you think she knows?" Mommy said, "I'll bet she does. I'll bet she's faking it, but that's okay."

So I ask them and they tell me. "Yes. There is no Santa, but don't tell Cookie. Santa is for little kids. You're growing up to be a big girl now."

I don't want to grow up. I want to grow down. I want there to be a real Santa. But I want to do what Mommy and Daddy tell me even if they tell me lies. Maybe they won't love me any more if I ask them about my real daddy. Did the car kill him right away? Did they take him to the hospital first? I wish I knew.

9. Dad's Roots

My stepfather, Everett, grew up in Portland, Maine, a city with a strong seafaring tradition. His father, Melvin, a flour merchant, sired three boys and three girls. The two daughters who never married remained in the family home. All three of the sons left. Stretching his gaze to the Atlantic Ocean from Casco Bay's high bluffs on the Western Promenade, Dad developed an early wanderlust, encouraged by his uncle, a Waldoboro farmer, who told him, "You'll die a fool if you never get to Boston." Eager to see the world, Everett left Dartmouth College in 1910 after three years and worked his way to Europe on a cattle boat. "I never took my shoes off for three weeks," he told us in his usual cryptic way.

In later years, he described his early life in a series of essays. The first began:

"Soon afterwards an opportunity to work in the Orient presented itself. It was December 24, 1915; I had been told to report to 26 Broadway, New York, offices of the Standard Oil Company of New York, to enter a training class for service in the Orient. A group of forty-five men had been selected from three hundred applicants. Most were recent college graduates from different parts of the country. Many held degrees in engineering – civil, electrical and mechanical. Supposedly these fields were crowded with little future. The opportunity to go to China at a salary of $2,000 a year, and sell kerosene oil for a period of three years, followed by a home leave of three months, seemed very attractive. The fact that we reported on the day before Christmas was of little concern; the chance to go to the Far East was not to be overlooked.

... Each Monday, we noticed that some of the men were missing. At the end of the training period, eighteen out of the original forty-five remained. Two were assigned to Java, [Indonesia] and the other sixteen to Shanghai, China. We considered ourselves lucky not to be sent to India or some other country."

Thus began Dad's Far-Eastern career in Shanghai. By 1938, when we lived in Manila, things were not going well at the family home in Maine. Dad's sister, Edith, took leave from her job at the Portland hospital records room to care both for father Melvin, who suffered from a weak heart, and also frail sister Annie, recovering from a broken bone. In his letters, Melvin blasted the Roosevelt administration. "The powers that be in Washington are out to get all they can to spend on their various schemes, most of them failures. The amount of graft and waste is enormous. The common man is being squeezed to pay the bill."

Away in the Merchant Marine, Dad's brother George, who spent most of his life on the open sea, wrote, "Wish I was able to give the girls, [Edith and Annie], a good liberal stipend as they should have and more than they have now. However, we are going along as usual and manage to keep out of the red."

The family was also trying to help their deceased brother Edwin's daughter. Sixteen-year-old Pat had recently been sentenced to three years in the women's reformatory in Skowhegan for shoplifting and prostitution. Mother wanted to help Pat, but Dad wrote "NO."

"I never knew that Henrietta [Pat's mother] was such a swine. I am finished with her and am sorry I sent I sent her $50 for Christmas. I shall put Pat and her mother out of my mind completely -- such a filthy mess. There was never anything like that in my family. I realize how it must have upset my father and sisters."

Although Everett judged his family harshly, they invariably showered Cookie and me with kindness. Constrained by hard times, they chose silver patterns for us and every Christmas sent sterling teaspoons for our trousseaus. Dad's sisters sent other gifts too: hand-knit mittens and caps, Big Chief lined paper tablets, rolls of Scotch tape. I would doodle away trying to dream up the obligatory thank-you notes, usually mentioning how the year had flown, I could hardly believe where it had gone. This to people in their sixties, seventies and eighties who wondered where on earth the decades had gone.

STANCO ordered Dad to leave Honolulu for a position at their New York headquarters in September of 1941. At 52, he would join the horde of expatriate managers moving to New York after lengthy careers in Oriental outposts. If Dad had any reservations, he never mentioned them in his letters.

As for Mother, she would be moving to the East Coast to live in the biggest city in the U.S. The long years of settling Hans Pederson's affairs were mostly over: his estate picked at by the conflicting claims of creditors, attorneys, charities, and also by his first wife Marie's relatives and friends. Now our mother had a husband, a Standard Oil man who adored her and their two small daughters, eight and four. I loved and respected my Dad Everett, but I look back now at the way he referred to people — not only foreigners, but members of his own family — and I cringe. He called them wops, scum, filth, and swine. Dad's harsh judgments must have influenced Mother's decision to say nothing about her early life. She rarely spoke of her Canadian family and never of her years in Seattle.

We were on our way to a new life after a stop in Maine to meet Dad's family. He was ready to put the expatriate years behind him. But Mom wasn't. She had married Everett to share his glamorous international life -- a life that was ending too soon.

When Cookie gave me my adoption paper two years after Mother died, I learned that it was during our 1941 hiatus in Portland that Dad adopted me. He waited for eight years until Hans Pederson's estate was settled. Because of the turmoil in Europe and the Far East, nobody knew if our home leave would be temporary. Six weeks later, when the Japanese bombed Pearl Harbor, my parents understood that our future was out of their hands.

———

I'm starting third grade at the Wayneflete School in Portland, because our family is staying with Grandfather and Daddy's sisters, Aunt Edith and Aunt Annie. Pretty soon we're going to move to New York. Out the window we see spruce trees on the sidewalk, so the street is called Spruce Street. Other trees have leaves that wave in the wind and shine in the sun. We climb the steep stairs to the second and third floors, because the Gibsons rent the first floor.

Aunt Edith and Aunt Annie wear long droopy dresses and thick brown stockings. Mommy says they are ugly. Aunt Annie rocks back and forth and sings off key when she plays the piano. Grandfather Melvin has our picture on the wall beside his desk, because that's the only way he could see us before we came to visit. His white mustache hangs down and makes him look sad. His eyes are red and watery, because he has heart trouble.

Aunt Edith works in the records room at the hospital. When she gets home she rushes around and cooks. She tells us what is wrong with everybody in Portland. Daddy told Mommy that Aunt Edith feels sorry for herself, because she had her breasts removed. Grandfather says she keeps the family together and is very good to our cousin Pat in jail. Daddy hates Pat. They all whisper about her. I hope they like me.

We sleep on the second floor behind the living room. My parents sleep on Grandpa's bed with Cookie's cot beside them. The rest of them have to climb the stairs to sleep on the third floor. Grandfather sleeps in Uncle George's bed, because Uncle George is away at sea in the Merchant Marine. I sleep in the sitting room. I love it! The chair beside my couch has china dolls with white faces, wearing beautiful lacy dresses that Grandmother made before she died. In the morning, the sun shines through the window and dust floats around the dolls like snow. The sewing basket on the table seems like China. Five Chinese kids with black pigtails wearing red suits are holding hands all around the pincushion.

Today Daddy and I walk on top of the high bluffs on the Western Promenade. His tie with blue stripes matches his blue suit. My dad's shoes are always shiny. He tells me I don't have to wear my dress-up Mary Janes, even though we're going out, because tie shoes are better for walking. I feel like a princess. This ocean has a salty smell, but it doesn't have beaches like Honolulu. The pine trees look like they're growing right out of the rocks. The boats go under the bridge with a "toot toot," and out toward the islands. Brown seaweed shows on the ledges when the tide is out.

Everyone is waiting for us at the top of the stairs when we get home from our walk. Grandfather takes my coat and hangs it on the coat tree. That walk was so fun for me, but what about Daddy? "I hope I didn't bore you today, Daddy," I say.

Why is everybody laughing?

10. Shallow Roots

In New York, we live in the Stanhope Hotel across the street from the Metropolitan Museum of Art until we can find our own apartment. The museum is my favorite place to play. Mommy holds our hands across Fifth Avenue with the smelly buses. We go up the stone steps to the huge hall and get our stickers at the desk, because we're members. Mom goes to the Asian Hall to study Chinese. Cookie and I turn right to the Egyptian Hall. Some mummies lie in their gold sarcophagus inside a pyramid. Other mummies are so small in their gray bandages. I tell Cookie about the hieroglyphics -- the little people on the wall who guard the mummies so they'll be safe. The mummies were kings. The hieroglyphic people have sideways legs and big shoulders looking frontwards.

Paula and Cookie 1943, 5th Avenue, New York.

Next we climb the wide staircase to the Medieval Hall, jumping on the steps to make echoes, then we play hide and seek around the knights in armor. I tell Cookie not to hide behind the big wall tapestries with forests. You never know, they might fall! My sister and I run up and down the stairs, because the knights might come clanking after us on their horses. I don't know how they can see with all that armor. We try to be quiet, so the guards won't notice us.

In the fourth grade our family moves to 90th Street and Madison Avenue, one block from Central Park. We only know the doorman and the elevator man who takes us up to our apartment on the eighth floor. In the elevator, people look straight ahead and never say anything. The wood floors have squares called parquet. Mommy hates the kitchen. It has an old black stove like the one at Grandfather's house in Portland. The maid's bathroom is filthy with soot, but we don't have servants, so nobody uses it except me sometimes when I have to hide. Daddy is always telling Mommy she's a wonderful cook. He says I should help her, but my mom just flops her hand and says no, the kitchen is hot and dirty. She tells me I'll learn to cook when I grow up, if I have to.

I take piano and read. I've read more books than anyone else in the fourth grade. My favorites are Freddie the Pig books. When Mommy and Daddy go out, I take care of Cookie. They want me to put her to bed, but she likes to wait up for me. Playing cards is not good, because I usually win and then she chews her pigtail the way she does when our parents talk too loud. Sometimes I make water bombs and we drop them out the window -- fast -- when I pull up the shade a little. Everyone in New York has blackout shades at night in case the Japs or the Nazis or the Wops try to bomb us.

I hope we never move again. The best thing is our school, Dalton. We hate weekends -- even vacations. Dalton seems like home. Most kids are Jewish, so Christians get scholarships. The teachers like to teach and they make us want to learn. They will always help us. Dalton is a progressive school, so starting in fifth grade, each teacher gives us a whole month of work at a time. It's our responsibility to get it done, so we keep a graph in our notebooks -- one for each subject. After we do the work, teachers color the graph with their special color. It ends up looking like a rainbow. We're doing fine. Especially Cookie. She reads even more books than I do. Daddy's afraid she'll need glasses.

On weekends, Daddy walks with us to the Central Park Zoo or the toy sailboat pond where the fathers launch boats with their kids. For lunch, we like to eat hamburgers and coconut cake at Hamburger Heaven. Sometimes I walk twenty or thirty blocks with my friends to the stores. FAO Schwartz has super-duper toys even though we've outgrown them. I roller skate too. One day I strap on my skates, tighten the skate key, and head uptown. I'm not supposed to go past 96th Street, because that's where the masses live. On 97th I run into some kids who start calling me a filthy, black Protestant. They chase me, but I skate home faster than they can run.

After school I practice the piano. Then Cookie and I listen to our radio programs, *Henry Aldrich, Captain Midnight,* and *Jack Armstrong, The All American Boy.* We collect Ovaltine box tops and send for a Jack Armstrong bombsight. We stand on chairs to bomb the Axis fleet on our rug. Cookie especially likes to save gum wrappers and roll big tin foil balls for the war effort.

Everyone has to be quiet at dinner because H.V. Kaltenborn and Edward R. Murrow talk on the radio about who's winning the battles. To do homework, sometimes I sit at Daddy's heavy mahogany wood desk in the living room. It has a big crack from when it was moved from China. If you cover the crack with papers, it doesn't hit you in the face like the crack in the glass door of Mother's curio cabinet where she keeps her jade birds and ivory Kuan Yin statues. That crack is like a jagged scar across the door. Mother's always saying, "I'll have to get it fixed."

Mostly the grownups are too busy listening to the news. They do their stuff and we do ours. We like Sunday nights the best. We climb into our beds, and Mommy brings us our supper on trays -- usually goldenrod eggs and fluffy snow pudding. It's our favorite dessert, but a lot of work for her to make. She has to beat all those egg whites turning the handle of that eggbeater until they stand straight up. Then she has to stir the yolks forever in a double boiler until they get thick for a custard sauce. She likes to make it for us though. We listen to our Sunday programs: *The Lone Ranger*, *The Shadow*, *Jack Benny*, and *Fred Allen*. One time I saw a picture of Fred and Gracie Allen. I didn't like it. It's more fun to imagine how people look.

Mom and Dad don't go out dancing the way they used to. They do not have many friends in New York. When the people who were stationed in China come over, they complain that those days are probably gone forever. When they have Mr. George, Daddy's boss, for dinner, he always says, "Lucky you didn't lose this fancy furniture when you were on home leave. Many men got robbed and looted. Cost the company a pretty penny."

The Georges don't have any kids, so they have no idea what to say to us. Mrs. George says stuff like, "Y'all are so pretty," and "Study hard in school, now."

Daddy is always quiet after they leave.

Our mother makes us dress up and curtsy when they come. I feel like a wind-up doll. A couple of times we've worn our hand-smocked dresses. Mommy bought each of us two of the same dress -- one pink and one blue. I got sick of alternating the same two dresses, but poor Cookie got stuck with all four of those dresses. She had to wear both of mine all over again after she outgrew hers.

Mom loves her furniture -- the carved roses on the beds with the yellow Philippine rice-cloth spreads embroidered with bamboo. She also hangs that stupid toilet picture of me on the wall between the beds. She stands back and admires her purple satin drapes. Ever since we used to play at the Metropolitan, she's decided all their China stuff is pricelessly antique.

One morning while Cookie gets ready for school, I bounce a tennis ball up onto the mantel by mistake and break Mom's Chinese wedding lamp. The big globe shatters and the stand breaks in half.

"You idiot! You stupid fool," my mother screams, and throws herself across her pink velvet couch. She cries and cries. On and on. Then it's "How I sacrifice for you."

I just feel numb. Here she goes again. I look at the flowers on the rug.

Amazingly, Mom stops. She blows her nose and hands me a dollar from her purse. "I've run out of cream for my coffee. Go get me a half pint at Gristedes."

I run to Gristedes and buy the cream. Cookie is hiding under the bed when I get home. She comes out when she hears me, and just stands there, scared, chewing her pigtail. I grab her coat, and we run all the way to Dalton. We don't talk the whole way, trying to forget about it. We never talk about it when Mommy yells at us or at Daddy.

We're late, but the nurse is still in the front hall. Every morning we walk past her when we come and open our mouths, so she can shine a light down our throats and send us home if we're sick. She's so nice. Her gray nurse uniform has a white collar and cuffs and her shoes are white too. We like Dalton, because people like us. The teachers like our work. I have a lot of friends there.

Sometimes I hate going home. Nothing I do is good enough at home. I guess Mom wonders whether I'm worth the sacrifice. She never cares about my schoolwork or my piano. Instead she says, "Why can't you be like Shirley Parsons?" Or, "Why can't you be like Barbara Henderson?"

Those kids, they're all rich. How am I supposed to be like them? I don't know. I don't think she knows either, except that they're supposed to be A-1 people. It's embarrassing when they come. Mother falls all over them with compliments and her phony voice. Then she pokes me as if I'm supposed to do it too. I wish she'd just be herself. I think Dalton kids are A-1 people too, but their parents didn't live in China. Besides, most of them are Jewish.

So, I set the table and do the dishes to help. One time, Mom comes home all mad, because I haven't fixed dinner. But if I try, she says, "Never mind. Enjoy your childhood. If you don't have maids, you'll learn to cook when you grow up."

On the other hand, she's always telling me, "You're so pretty." I hate it. It doesn't make me feel pretty. It makes me feel as if I'm some Christmas ornament hanging on the tree. What if I had an accident and wasn't pretty anymore? I bet she'd hide me in the closet. Daddy's not much better. He's always telling Mother, "Look what you produced." All they care about is how I look. Well, I think how you act and what you think is more important. Cookie seems to stay out of their way and read.

Sometimes I talk back to Mom, but not to Dad. We get along fine, because I just tell him, "Yes Daddy," and then do as I please. He's glued to the radio all the time, especially to hear what's going on in the Pacific Theater of the war.

11. Spreading Roots

Boy am I glad we don't have to spend the summer in New York. Nobody at Dalton stays in the city. Most kids go to camp so they won't get polio. You'd never dare go to a public swimming pool, they're always warning you about that. Sometimes polio isn't so bad, but some people get paralyzed and end up in an iron lung. It's scary. Dad drives us to Maine for the summer. In the winter in New York City, we take the bus or the subway or even a taxi, so we leave the car in a garage all winter. We save our gas rationing coupons for the trip to Maine.

Dad found a resort hotel on the coast where Mom, Cookie and I can stay all summer. It's our second year there. It takes two days to drive there, because the speed limit is thirty-five miles an hour during wartime. We read the Burma Shave signs along the highway:

"His cheek was rough

His chick vamoosed.

And now she won't

Come home to roost

Burma Shave"

The first night we stop at a tourist home in the Berkshires. We don't go to those fancy hotels where the bellhops wear tuxes and you have to tip them when they carry your suitcase. The next day we drive to Maine. We stop for dinner at Lamie's Tavern in New Hampshire. Then we get to Maine and drive through all these little towns on coastal Route 1 -- York, Wells, Ogunquit. We read more Burma Shave signs:

"To kiss a mug

That's like a cactus

Takes more nerve

Than it does practice

Burma Shave"

Someone told Dad about this new kind of place out west you can stay in called a motel. You drive your car right up to the door of your room and carry in your own suitcases. "Keep your eyes peeled for a motel," Dad tells us, but we haven't seen one yet. All we see are Burma Shave signs.

We stay a couple of days in Portland with Aunt Edith, Aunt Annie, and Uncle George. He's retired from the Merchant Marine, so now he's a desk clerk at an inn in Boothbay Harbor. It's fun to hear him talk. Whenever our uncle goes some place he likes, he'll say, "Gorry, it was a real whiz-bang."

We play the piano for Aunt Annie. Then she plays for us, swaying and screeching while she floors the pedal. They save their meat coupons for when we come, and Aunt Edith cooks huge roasts. If we stay over a Saturday night, we have baked beans and brown bread. Aunt Edith knows a good bean baker. She takes her bean pot over in the morning, and he bakes it all day for her to pick up that night. I love that spicy smell and the soft dark bread.

Mom is always in a hurry to leave. "Look at their drab clothes and ugly shoes," she says. They know she's a snob. It hurts their feelings when they are so good to us. Daddy always likes nice clothes, but he would never say anything because they are his sisters.

We stay in Portland long enough to get gold fillings from Dr. Woods, Dad's dentist. He's mostly retired now, but he does us since Dad was his first patient. He never uses Novocain. "If I hit a nerve I want to know it," he says every year. Boy, do I know it! First he drills, and then he squirts in the cold air. Then he swabs the cavity with iodine or something before he fills it. It's awful, but it's only once a year. Dad tells him he's better than any big city dentist.

When Dr. Woods is done, we drive up the coast to the resort. Most guests come for one, two, or even four weeks, but we stay all summer. Dad stays a few days before he takes the train back to New York. "You weren't born here so you'll never be a native," he tells us. "You're from away." He likes to stand around with his hands in his pockets, swaying back and forth and talking to the year-round people, None of them say much. "They don't waste words up here," he says.

I wish our dad could stay too. He loves to hike and take us out in the boat and play golf, but he has to work. After his vacation in August, he drives us back in time for school. Why should they send us to camp when Mother can stay here too and play golf and tennis and swim where it's cool? She is so happy here. Since we stay all summer, we live in the cheapest room -- the one under the bowling alley where the pins crash when they fall. We get used to it though. It doesn't keep us awake.

Mother loves Maine. We are VIPs here. Everyone knows us because we stay all summer. We have our own table in the dining room by the door so everyone talks to us when they go in and out. Mom is proud of us up here. We seem to be A-1 people, because we live in New York City.

My friends up here have their own cottages. After breakfast we go out and play and hardly see our parents until dinner. I roam through the woods with my sister. We swim in the bay, or at the beach, or the saltwater pool. We buy ice cream at the snack bar. At night, besides candlepin and duckpin bowling just above our ceiling, there is bingo and horse races with wooden horses that get moved when they roll the dice. We kids are the jockeys. Our resort has square dancing, movies, ballroom dancing, and Sunday night community sings. Cookie and I spend so much time at the pool that they let us join the waitresses' water ballet troupe. Even Cookie. She's little, but she's a graceful star with her nice long legs.

Since we're here all summer, I set up tasks for myself. I run up and down the mountain every morning before breakfast. It's really not a mountain, just a high ledge that takes about a half hour to climb to the top. Then you see the view of all the islands. Sometimes I slow down like I'm in a primeval forest. With all the moss and ferns, you half expect a dinosaur, or at least a moose, to round the corner. One morning a moose actually did stand in the lake and eat lily pads for breakfast. I take Cookie with me when she wants to come.

We share our boat with the Hastings. Their kids, Carolyn and Bruce, are about our age, but I'm the oldest. One day we find a Coke bottle on the ping-pong table at the bowling alley, so we go to a bathroom and play spin the bottle. It's boring because Bruce is the only boy and he's just turned seven.

Then we go to Mrs. Carpenter's gift shop. Bruce and Carolyn have already bought most of the kids' stuff, but we look it over anyway. One shelf looks different. It has two figurines on it just like the ones Mom got from my real father -- a little girl in a blue dress and a little boy in overalls smoking his father's pipe. They are so cute.

"Where's your mother?" Mrs. Carpenter asks.

"She's playing golf with Mrs. H. and Jim and Bob." Those guys always come for two weeks.

Mrs. Carpenter rearranges the jewelry.

Next we go to the lighthouse. It only looks like a lighthouse; it's really just rooms for the guests. The sign on the door says *children under sixteen must be accompanied by an adult.*

"C'mon. Let's go," I tell the kids. So we climb the stairs to the observation deck on the top floor. Nobody is there, so we run around on the window seats for a while. After that, we go down the causeway to the point. At the boathouse, we see the saddest thing, two dead kittens in the corner. Their little teeth show because their mouths are open. We decide to have a burial at sea. We get a cigar box at Carolyn's house, and we make chain necklaces out of daisies for the kittens. Their necks are stiff when we put the necklaces on. Carolyn puts one of Daddy's handkerchiefs into the cigar box so they'll have a bed.

We borrow our dads' boat that they share. Cookie and Ben can't swim very far, so I make them put on the life jackets under the seat. I'm not sure how to start the motor, but I yank the cord a few times, and it finally kicks in. I steer the boat out in the bay. It slaps the rough water, because we're all sitting in the stern. I tell Carolyn to move up to the bow with the cigar box. I grab hold of a lobster buoy, but the boat only slows down a little. We say our prayer, "Now I lay me down to sleep." Carolyn drops the cigar box off the bow.

Then it gets horrible. The box is supposed to sink to the bottom, but instead, the lid opens and the kittens float away. Their daisy necklaces fall apart. I hold on to the lobster buoy, but the boat keeps going. We don't stick around to see how long the kittens will float. I just point the boat back to the dock. We bang into it, but Carolyn jumps out and ties the rope to a cleat. Then we go back to our room and eat Oreo cookies for lunch. It was awful watching those dead kittens float away in the cold gray water.

I think about those figurines in the gift shop. All of a sudden I know that they really are my real father's figurines. When I ask Mother, she admits it.

"They were my father's. How can you sell them?" For a change, I'm the one who gets mad. I cry and I yell. I can't help it.

"Okay, okay. Calm down. I'll get them back."

She sounds disgusted. Then I remember about the silverware. She has her Chantilly sterling like the spoons Aunt Annie and Aunt Edith give us every Christmas for our trousseaus. She uses her sterling for good. But for every day we use the silverware with the "P" on it. One time when I was wiping it dry. I asked if the "P" was for Pederson.

"Yes," she said, with a kind of ugh. She grabbed the forks and threw them into the drawer.

Since Mom wants to get rid of my father's stuff, I think maybe she'd like to get rid of me too. Sometimes she gives me this dirty look, and I think, "What did I do?" It's as if she's mad at me for being alive. It might be something to do with my real father, but she gets mad at Cookie too. We never know what to do. She can be so nice sometimes, but she just can't seem to stop yelling and crying.

I know she and Dad take good care of us. They send us to Dalton, so we won't have to go to public school with the masses. We go to Maine, so we won't have to swim in the New York public pools and get polio.

12. Deeper Roots

I guess Mother felt badly about the figurines, because when we get back to New York, she tells me they are Royal Copenhagen and I can have them when I grow up. Whenever Mom and Dad go out, I go in their room and pick the figurines up off her bureau. The little girl is sucking her thumb. She's an okay little girl like me, I guess. She has short hair with bangs like I have in that toilet picture they keep between their beds. But the little boy! He's like a chubby little three-year-old toddler. You can tell his overalls are kind of baggy even though the figurine is porcelain or whatever it's made of. The overalls are too big, just like when Mom sometimes buys us clothes to grow into, especially huge coats, like we're poor or something. That little boy is leaning over smoking a pipe like he knows he shouldn't do it but he's doing it anyway. Personality. Underneath these figurines there is a crown and it has the word Copenhagen. Well, Copenhagen is in Denmark. My father's name was Hans Pederson, so even though I was born in Seattle, maybe he was Danish. Maybe he went back to Denmark to get away from us after I was born, and the car killed him there.

Mother tells us how lucky we are to live in a good home where we have enough money. One day she told us about living with her sister and brother when they were students. "One time I only had twenty five cents, she said. "So I bought a quart of strawberries, and we ate strawberries and cream."

It must have been scary for her after my father got run down by a car and left her penniless with me to raise. She hardly ever talks about when she was a little girl in Canada except for the hard winters. They ate food from the root cellar. One time she said she has bunions and corns on her feet, because growing up she had to wear hand-me-down shoes. I'm really sorry she's had such a hard life. I know we are so lucky.

Sometimes, these thick letters come in the mail. "Here's a letter from Padden and Moriarty," Dad says, and hands it to Mother. They are both so happy when she opens the letter. One time I asked who Padden and Moriarty were.

"My lawyers in Seattle," she said.

She has a picture album up in her closet that she showed me once. There is a beautiful picture of her in front of some trees the year she was voted Miss Edmonton. The photos are mostly of me, because it's my baby book. When I was a baby, the rule was that you weren't supposed to pick up your babies when they cried, because you would spoil them and they wouldn't learn routines. She said she hated that rule. She always picked me up and cuddled me. "You were such a sweet little baby," she said.

154

Some pictures show my Aunt Alice holding me outdoors on the fire escape in Seattle. I like to visit Aunt Alice in New Hampshire on vacations. She's easygoing. She sews clothes for me and teaches me to sew. I play with her little girl, Diane. She's so cute. She's six years younger than I am. Sometimes Aunt Alice asks me what I want to be when I grow up.

I always say, "Oh, a garbage collector, I guess." One time I said this when she was hanging out the laundry. Diane and Cookie and I lay on the grass together taking a sunbath while the sheets flapped in the fresh-smelling breeze.

Aunt Alice took a clothespin out of her mouth. "You can be something better than that. You can be anything you want. You can probably even be a princess," she said.

1936 Shanghai: Paula (2), Aunt Alice (24)

155

She sounds like my parents. But sometimes both my mother and my dad make me feel like garbage. If I do decide to be a garbage collector, it will be my own choice. I won't have to worry any more about looking pretty all the time and being such a hotshot A-1 person.

In seventh grade I start to grow up. I'm not ready for this. For one thing, I'm getting breasts. We all wear these cardigan sweaters with matching grosgrain ribbon along the edge that we button up the back. Well. My friends start teasing me because my breasts bounce around when we run up and down the school stairs.

"You need a bra," my friend Susie says.

Easy for her to say, she's still flat. I tell Mother. She goes out and buys some. "See if these fit your boobs," she says, and dumps them on my bed. I don't like the way they bind across my back. I don't think my mother likes me to be needing a bra.

Just before Christmas, she begins telling Cookie and me all about how we're going to be getting the best Christmas present ever. All she talks about is how we will love our Christmas presents. Each one is in a long narrow box under the tree, beautifully wrapped in gold paper.

Cookie opens hers first. It's a bridesmaid doll in a yellow organdy dress, sleeping in her box inside tissue paper. I guess Cookie likes it all right; it's a beautiful doll for an eight-year-old.

Then Mother picks up my box and brings it over to me. I open my eyes wide so I'll look excited, but I have a sinking feeling about what's coming, and I'm right. Inside the box is a bride doll in the most beautiful swirly white dress, lying in her tissue-paper bed like the sleeping beauty waiting for her prince or something.

"Oh, how beautiful. Thank you so much," I say. For heaven's sake, I'm twelve years old. Way too old for dolls.

Then, right after Christmas, Nancy, April, and Susie come over one day after school. I bring out Cokes and brownies that Mother always makes for my friends. She knows Nancy can't resist them because Nancy's mother never bakes. They sit in a row on Cookie's bed facing me. I straddle the piano stool and hook my legs around the edges. I guess my underpants show under my skirt. They keep looking at each other. April keeps pressing her hand to her mouth. Finally, she says, "I think you've started."

I turn beet red. We've never talked about this stuff. I am mortified. Nobody knows what to say so they all get up and leave. They must be wrong. I go to the bathroom and look. I decide it must be dried diarrhea in my underpants, except it's a different color. More of a purple. I've heard about this, but I didn't think it would happen for a couple of years. I'm the first one in our group.

I tell Mother, but she doesn't say anything. I go in the bathroom and keep wiping myself with toilet paper and looking at the blood. I wonder if I'm bleeding to death. That night when I'm in the bathroom, I hear Dad walk into the bedroom. He opens my bureau drawer, and tosses something into the drawer. When I open the drawer, I see a box of Kotex and a sanitary belt box. I read the directions and use them. Maybe my parents are more embarrassed than I am, because they never mention it again. Maybe they wish I'd keep playing with dolls.

A couple of days later, Susie invites us to her house after school. Her father is a doctor. He's bought her this book with diagrams about reproduction. She spreads it out on her bed. We lean on her ruffled bedspread and read about that stuff.

"Great. Pretty soon we can have babies," Nancy says. "Just what we need."

I don't want to think about it. I guess Mother did that reproduction stuff with my real father to have me as a baby. Maybe that's why she won't talk about him.

I go home more after school now. I do scales and arpeggios to strengthen my hands, because I'm learning Chopin's *Polonaise Militaire*. We have a lot of homework in seventh grade. Instead of getting together, my friends and I talk on the phone. The hall phone has a long extension cord, so I take it to the storeroom for privacy. I sit in the dark and lean against the beat-up wardrobe trunks with all those labels from where we used to live before the war.

"Stop monopolizing the phone," Mom and Dad tell me, although they hardly ever get any calls. Some of my friends have their own extension phones, but that's expensive. We're always trying to save money. If we forget to turn out the lights when we leave the room, Dad says, "I don't work for the electric company." Makes sense. It's another story at the cottage we rent in Maine now. It's cheaper than staying at the resort, because we fix our own food. I never talk on the phone in Maine. Up there it's all four-party lines. We can hear our neighbors breathe when we're on the phone.

We have dance and drama in school. I was a dancer in Stravinsky's *Petrouchka*. When we put on Shakespeare's *The Tempest*, I

was the first half of Prospero's daughter, Miranda. My opening speech
was,

> "If by your art,
>
> My dearest father,
>
> You have put the wild waters in this roar,
>
> Allay them."

Mother always comes to the performances. For *The Tempest,* she
wore her black satin cocktail suit with pink stripes and her lacy Tatiana
hat from Saks Fifth Avenue. None of the other parents were so dressed
up. Her outfit was beautiful, but I think she felt funny. I tried to get her
to join my friends' parents, but she mostly talked to me.

Another thing I do after school now is Episcopal confirmation
class at the Church of the Heavenly Rest right around the corner on
Fifth Avenue. Since I don't know those kids, I've been trying to get
someone from Dalton to get confirmed with me. Carrot-topped Brigit
Moynihan is Catholic. So is Inez De Torres. I think that Inez, her
brother Juan, and their mother are refugees from the Spanish Civil
War. They stick to themselves. The only other Christian in my class is
Maddie, but her family isn't religious. Her father calls us "The Church
of the Heavily Dressed," but he said Maddie could come to
confirmation class.

Maddie and I have summer birthdays so we never have
birthday parties. The Park Avenue kids usually have about half the class
to their parties. When we were younger, we'd have ice cream and cake,
then take taxis to the Barnum and Bailey Circus. Now they take us to
Broadway matinees -- *Oklahoma!, Annie Get Your Gun,* and *Brigadoon.*

————

Thank God the war is finally over. The veterans are home and some of them are coming to teach at Dalton. But they don't stay long. We've had three English teachers this year. First we had this singing guy, Mr. Seeger, who played his guitar. Then we had Mrs. Hiss, poor lady. We tried to do what she said, because her husband, Alger, went through some kind of trial with Whittaker Chambers. I'm afraid they went to jail. Senator Joseph McCarthy thinks they are Communists.

Then we get this English teacher, Johnson. He's a veteran and extremely handsome. He gets us to read challenging books. I just finished *Tom Jones*, by Henry Fielding. It's a big nineteenth century novel with dirty parts. We get extra credit for hard books and we're getting a crash course in grammar too, since we've never had it. Johnson tells us we can pick up grammar by osmosis if we read a lot. We have vocabulary tests too. One week we had to define the word "sporadic."

When Johnson handed the tests back, he said, "It means scattered -- in one sense only. You might hear sporadic gunfire. But the word is not used as one student wrote in his sentence, 'The man fell off the building and was sporadic.'"

I hadn't thought about my real father for a while. The last time the subject came up, Mom told me that the Depression was so awful that men sold apples in the street and jumped off of buildings. I wonder if that happened to my father. Maybe he was so upset when I was born that he jumped off a building and landed scattered on the sidewalk.

The thing of it is, I've fallen in love with Johnson. I'm not the only one. Oh boy, the way he looks at me: I love his crooked smile. The other day I was speaking to him at his desk about *Tom Jones*. All of a sudden he reaches over to my sweater and pulls off a piece of lint or something from just above my boobs. I can't even describe the way it made me feel. I know I blushed. I felt this tingling all over my body. I felt like maybe I was wetting my pants or something, except it wasn't pee. I couldn't even talk. I looked at the floor, but when I looked back up at him, he looked down at the papers on his desk.

So, now I only talk to him with my friends. They love him too. Nancy found out where he lives, so on weekends we walk over to his Third Avenue brownstone where he has an apartment. Susie took a picture of Nancy and me standing on his steps with our hands in prayer position. One day we saw his wife coming home from shopping, so we hid behind some cars across the street. Her coat was old and shapeless, and she wore her hair in a bun. We were amazed. We thought she'd be some glamour puss with a long pageboy like Rita Hayworth. But then everyone knows that teachers don't make much money.

13. Uprooted

In late 1946, Dad went to China on a freighter via Panama in order to transport Mother's fortieth birthday investment – a maroon Buick that he hoped to sell in Shanghai for $10,000. Auto manufacturers had reconfigured their wartime assembly lines to meet the pent-up consumer demand for cars. "I have full confidence in you as a natural businesswoman and I'm sure the years ahead will be as good and better than those behind us," Dad wrote Mother optimistically from the freighter.

He changed his mind when he reached Shanghai. Chaos reigned on the docks. Furniture disappeared. Trunks were broken open and the contents stolen. Thievery was rife as Mao's Communists moved in on Chiang Kai-shek's Nationalist citizens. Even though Dad had been telling himself for five years that his expat career had probably ended, he must have hoped he would be wrong. Post-war Shanghai jolted him into reality. He had counted on making a good profit on the sale of Mother's car to maintain her confidence. But far from home, he began to doubt his future.

Afraid to drive Mom's car, because he couldn't match the paint if it were damaged, Dad tried to sell it right away. He noticed about fifty Buicks on the docks, and realized that his $10,000 price was too high. After his efforts to keep the maroon paint intact, he eventually sold the car for $7,000 to a government official who had it painted black. Worried, he wrote Mother:

"I hope you don't feel too bad because I have not been able to do better with your car … I hope you do not get too independent of not having a man around. I certainly need a wife and miss you very much. I will do my best to prove useful when I get back."

Mother's rootless life had not provided her with an idea of where to live next. While she had just turned forty, Dad was fifty-eight, I was thirteen and Cookie nine. Several years would pass before we were grown. Seeing an uncertain future ahead, Mother offered to join Dad in China. He responded,

"You seem much concerned about what I will do when I get back, Sweetie. I would say there is no possibility of our going to China to live. The business is not there with present restrictions. Even whiskey, cigars, cigarettes, Coca Cola cannot be imported now. Cosmetics are prohibited. Further, as to what I do when I get back, I am not concerned. I don't think I want any more STANCO export. Might get something better in [Standard Oil of] Jersey or New York -- it couldn't be worse than STANCO. If they want to retire me I don't mind. Will be in business for myself somewhere and that will be somewhere where you like. In my opinion, Maine has big possibilities in the real estate business. I don't like winters there either. Anyway, I will be working at something."

Still, Mother kept offering to come. He told her: "The money in Shanghai is all gone to hell and the situation is acute making the import business impossible. Prices: toast, $600. Glass of fresh milk, $2,000. I carry a suitcase of money to work with me every day."

Dad had another problem. Although he kept STANCO advised of his movements, he heard nothing from them. Traveling to Batavia, Java [Indonesia -- still a Dutch colony], he found conditions no better.

"There is little I can do here because of the trouble in Java. The Dutch hold a few coast cities, but the interior is in the hands of the rebel natives. They are supposed to have more than 25,000 Jap soldiers with them and they are all well armed. I think there will have to be a lot of fighting before the situation is normal, maybe several years. Batavia is crowded with Dutch from Holland and also refugees from the interior. Palembang is now quiet, but the oil fields are in native hands.

I have had no word from NY since I left so am traveling as I see fit. I will have had enough traveling when I finish with this trip. Except for Shanghai, it is necessary to share a hotel room with somebody else. In Hong Kong they had no mattress the first night and I slept on boards. Here the first night I slept in a child's bed with my feet stretched out."

Dad's repeated letters and expense account filings to STANCO's export department went unanswered for four months. The company was in the middle of a management shakeup. Dad's boss,

Larry George, was fired. This was fine with Dad who felt George had never stood up for his men. He continued to reassure Mother.

"I would say there is no possibility of our going to China to live, Sweetie. There is the devil to pay over the dollar situation. Dealings in American dollars are prohibited. Offices have been raided. They search passengers arriving and leaving to see how many American dollars they have. Only 100 are allowed. All they think about is how to get another loan from America. It would be like throwing dollars into the ocean.

Finally heard from STANCO. They are considering some special compensation for me. Booking passage to come home. I will be looking for you when I arrive in San Francisco and will try to be looking my best."

―――――――

While Daddy travels in China, their Premier, Chiang Kai-shek is having problems. I miss Dad, but we keep busy here. In eighth grade we're getting ready for high school next year. We're doing pre-Latin. Mother won a contest for a week at Elizabeth Arden's Red Door Spa. I think she's the star, because the other women are fat -- still they all have to eat the special detox diet. She's brought home a slant board and lies on it with her feet higher than her head and compresses on her eyes, all to go along with her makeover and cosmetics. She's out a lot at night too sometimes after we're in bed, because she takes Chinese Art courses at Columbia. It's funny how she reads so slowly, moving her finger along the line and reading with her lips like a foreigner learning English or something.

166

She never says much about Daddy's letters from China. But one time she brought up my real father again, mentioning that huge oil painting in the gold frame above the couch. It reaches almost to the ceiling. It's a painting of a village, Lillehammer, in Norway. This peasant woman is walking along partly in shadows formed on either side of the road by high snow banks. I love it. It's so peaceful. Mother said my real father bought it from the Danish Consul General in Seattle when the consul was called back to Copenhagen. King Christian of Denmark has the only other snow scene this artist painted. I guess it's a pretty famous and valuable painting. I'm glad Mother inherited it since she had such a struggle after my father died.

Still, sometimes I wonder. He had that painting, and the Royal Copenhagen figurines, and the sterling lily-of-the-valley demitasse spoons. Since he didn't have any money, he probably gave Mother those nice things so she could take care of me. I guess he thought she could sell them if she had to.

Daddy has this great STANCO job. Now that it's April, he's finally coming home. Mother just left on the train for San Francisco to meet him. Aunt Helen, her other sister from Canada, is staying with us. She's a teacher. She sounds just like Aunt Alice with her pretty Canadian voice.

"What I like best are stories," Aunt Helen says. "I like to tell the children about the old days when your mother and I were children. I live in Edmonton now, but we grew up on a farm. We grew vegetables and kept them in the root cellar to eat in winter. Since we didn't have electricity or a refrigerator, we lowered a rope down the well to keep our bucket of butter and cheese cool. Our family always ate cottage cheese."

"We eat cottage cheese too," I tell her. "Mother says it's good for us."

"Oh yes. It is." Aunt Helen is sitting on Mother's pink velvet couch mending one of my socks. She stretches the heel over a darning egg just like Aunt Edith and Aunt Annie do in Portland.

"I'll bet it was cold," I said. "Like that." I point to the Lillehammer painting.

"Of course. Canada is very cold in winter. But we had a sleigh and horses to pull us through the snow."

Aunt Helen makes little stitches through my sock. I wonder if it will rub on my heel and give me a blister.

She twists her neck to look over her shoulder. "That painting is very much like Canada in winter." Her glasses slide down her nose when she turns to look at me. One earpiece is held on by a safety pin. "I remember that painting very well. It was in your father's apartment when I visited your mother in Seattle before you were born."

All of a sudden I really want her to go on. I don't say a word.

She cocks her head to the side. "Your father was such a kind, jolly man. And his art collection! Why they lived in a double penthouse. They needed the entire top floor of the apartment building to display his paintings."

"I'd better do some homework." I jump up and head for my room. I don't know what to think. Aunt Helen says my father was a nice man who lived in a penthouse. I always thought he was mean and horrible, because he became poor in the Depression. I'll bet Mother had to sell his paintings after he died so we wouldn't starve. I guess she kept the Lillehammer painting, because it was the biggest one. It was probably the most valuable since it has that thick gold frame with all the curlicues like you see in museums. Maybe she didn't want the other paintings since she's so stuck on all her Chinese stuff.

Daddy will be home soon, and we'll be so glad to see him. He wrote me a letter and said, *"You should see me after the middle of April so be looking your best when I get there."* Guess I'll wear my draggy new skirt that swirls around my ankles and weighs a ton. I feel like I'm wearing a blanket. Mother's gone all out on our wardrobes so we'll have the "new look." Just for once though, I wish my parents would stop worrying about how people look all the time.

Actually, I want to look nice too. Mother took me shopping to buy a couple of formals for Miss Bloss's tea dances. I started going with Maddie. At first Mother said no, it's too expensive. Then Paul Furstenburg invited me to a dance at Temple Emmanuel. She wouldn't let me go. At the tea dances, we have to wear white gloves and fill out our dance cards with tassels down the center. Maddie and I are the only ones from Dalton. The other girls are from Nightingale Bamford, Chapin, and Brearley. The boys go to Trinity and Collegiate. They never want to dance. They hide in the bathroom until Miss Bloss goes in and drags them over to the refreshment table. I'm not much of a hit with them. I never know what to say. Maybe it's my frilly formals. Maddie has this knockout red and purple taffeta plaid dress. The boys

169

dance with her. She rocks her elbow up and down and clucks in their ear while they do the box step. Maybe I should try that.

14. Moving to Maine

It's 1949, and Daddy's, retiring because there's no more business in China. He's been at loose ends around the house waiting for school to end. I guess Maine is as good as anywhere, if we have to leave New York and Dalton. A switch might not be bad. I'm just finishing tenth grade, so it's an awkward time for me, but it's a good time for Cookie as she's ending sixth and will be starting junior high. We are all consumed with the rush of wrapping up our lives in New York. It's good to have these moving projects, it keeps my mind off this wrenching loss of leaving my really good friends of seven years.

Cookie and I board the train headed to New Hampshire to stay with Aunt Alice while Mom and Dad move our stuff. I watch as the city I've grown to love disappears and the heavy awareness of leaving friends behind brings the sting of tears. Spring greens flash by as the train rattles its way north, a welcome change after the dulled hues of midtown Manhattan. At one stop, I exit the train and find my sadness lifted by the fresh fragrance of lilacs. I may survive this move after all I realize, as we pass dots of popping color, that a clean slate at a new school will offer a new start.

I'm excited because, Aunt Alice is making me a cute dress, not too long and very stylish. She's a meticulous seamstress. I love the detailed trim she's sewn around the keyhole neckline. and the peplum ruffle at the waist. I tell her she should be a dress designer, but I'll probably still be a garbage collector. She laughs. It's a nice, lilting laugh that makes me appreciate how well she understands my humor compared to other adults.

She gets down on her knees to check the length of my dress with a yardstick. Her shiny brown hair is always in an upsweep -- sophisticated looking even though she lives in the country. She stands up and hugs me. "You're much too pretty to be a garbage collector."

I turn back and forth in front of the mirror. "You sound like my parents. Maybe I'll marry one instead. Garbage collectors deserve pretty wives too." I can say whatever I want when I'm with Aunt Alice. It's comforting. I love to visit her and play with her cute daughter Diane. Cousin Diane is nine now. Mostly she plays with Cookie, who's eleven, while I watch Aunt Alice. She's teaching me how to sew, taking my mind off of the impending changes in our lives.

My parents have bought an old house to remodel on the coast of Maine. It's sweet that Dad wants us to have a chance to live in a house with a yard instead of a city apartment. We have three wooded acres all the way down to Casco Bay, and our own little beach with a float. It's a welcome change; I'm carried away with the romance of living near the water and having room to roam. We've inherited some chickens. Mom knows how to take care of them, because she grew up on a farm. She throws kitchen scraps over the wire, and they peck them right up, especially the tomatoes. We're even growing our own tomatoes.

"How about some flowers?" I ask.

"No thanks," Mother says. "I don't intend to dig in the dirt any more than I have to." You'd think she hates exercise, but my mom is as slim and energetic as ever.

"Besides, you'll just have to water them and then they'll die," Dad adds, frowning his thick brows together. Cousin Diane calls him Uncle Bushy Brows. He's happily busy supervising the remodeling — sweeping up after the carpenters leave and spackling nail holes.

September arrives all too quickly and it's time for me to leave for boarding school. I head for Abbot Academy, the oldest girls' school in New England. I have a scholarship, so I'm working hard. I like it, though it's totally different from Dalton. They've added gracious living to the tough academics to refine us. The regimen requires daily chapel right after breakfast. To keep us abreast of world events and teach us poise, each student is assigned a week to report world news to the entire school at chapel. I find this nerve racking and see that other girls feel the same way. You have to stand in front of everyone holding your index cards, trying not to let your hands shake. Classes go straight through morning until we break at 11:00 a.m. for tiffin, a genteel word for snack. We generally have cake or cookies to ramp up our energy. On cold days we have consommé and crackers just like the tiffin I remember having on the big ocean liners.

173

After lunch we have sports — usually hockey or basketball. In beginning tennis, we don't spend much time actually hitting the ball over the net. First we learn to pick up the ball in a ladylike manner — placing it against the inside of the left foot, then scooping it up with the racquet, so we don't have to -- *gasp* -- bend over. For dinner we are expected to dress in a slightly better outfit, usually a sweater, skirt and stockings. Nobody wears a girdle or a garter belt; we just pull on old, runny stockings then roll them and twist them just below our knees like twenties flappers.

Abbot is in the town of Andover where there's a big boys' academy that I learn is one of the best prep schools on the east coast. The schools go to great lengths to keep us apart, but sometimes the boys' academy has tea dances. Abbot monitors our mail for unauthorized communication. If we get a letter postmarked Andover, we're called to the office and made to read it aloud to make sure it's an invitation to a tea dance. If it isn't, who knows? Maybe you're expelled for receiving a love letter. Dances are exciting, but they are also intimidating. When Abbot hosts dances we use those old-fashioned dance cards with the tassels down the center. Boys we don't even know have to fill them out to reserve dances. I'm still not much good at talking to boys.

They play Dixieland music a lot at our dances, and I've picked up the Charleston. On a Saturday leave to Boston, I found a raccoon coat for $3.00. The thing is, most public school kids do the Jitterbug, not the Charleston. They don't play the Jitterbug at Abbot or Andover. Maybe they're afraid some guy with a duck-tailed haircut might show up in a Zoot suit and try to teach us the Lindy. When the dances are over, we file out with our last dance partner, shake hands with the headmistress, and go our separate ways. For heaven's sake! We're in the middle of 1950!

Mom and Dad are settling into Maine, but it isn't easy. Dad's not an A-1 Standard Oil man any more. Starting all over with an old house to remodel has taken its toll on Mom. Dad has a job as a stockbroker in the Portland Merrill Lynch office, but it isn't like selling in China where his agents provided automatic customers. Mother keeps nagging, "Call people up. You know how to invest. Look what you've done with my stocks." Dad is too proud to cold call folks. Mom and Dad don't really know anyone here and Dad is realizing that it takes connections to gain trust with the circumspect New Englanders. I can tell Dad is distressed even though he says it will all work out. He's clearly worried the job is about to fizzle.

On a cheerful note, Mom is happy using her creativity to remodel the house. She put blue Chinese wallpaper with huge pink peonies in the front hall and living room. When she gave a neighborhood tea and wore the golden silk kimono Dad brought her from China, the party rated a front-page photo in the society section of *The Portland Press Herald*. Now she feels a bit foolish at making such a big deal out of the party, realizing that nearly everyone with an old house in Maine has authentic antiques and colonial wallpaper. Mom feels out of place surrounded by staid New Englanders. When she wore her black and pink striped satin suit and her doily-style Tatiana hat to a Christmas party, the other women had on tweed suits and sensible flat-heeled shoes. "They're about as stylish as your sisters," she told Dad.

We joined St. Mary's Episcopal Church. I hope it helps Mom make some nice friends. At the midnight Christmas Eve service, I got dizzy and sweaty. "I'm going to sit in the car," I whispered to Dad. Pretty soon he joined me in the back seat. He placed his arm gently around my shoulders and draped his fingers lightly down my arm. It was such a tender moment. I felt like he really loved me. I wonder if my real father would have loved me the way Everett does. I can't imagine a better dad than Everett.

Dad has developed a leg problem. He drags one leg when he climbs the stairs. He's sixty-eight now, and Mother is only fifty. If I get married at twenty-two that would make my husband forty! Most of my friends parents are only a few years apart in age. I'm beginning to realize that Mom is unusual. I didn't know how unusual until many years later when I discovered that her first husband, my father Hans, was old enough to be her grandfather. No wonder his family was wary of Mother's motives. Hastily marrying a woman decades younger than he was must have seemed suspicious to them, especially given his rapidly declining health.

Dad is depressed and Mother's crabby. Their neighbors, who are all older like Dad, bought their houses years ago for a song. We're having trouble keeping up with them, because their children are grown, but Cookie and I are still in the expensive years. Cookie goes to public school now like most American kids. Sometimes I wish I did too. I've gone to private school my whole life. Cookie's school seems okay, but Mother and Dad feel guilty about it. I'll bet they send Cookie to Abbot after I graduate. She's smarter than I am, so I'm sure she'll get a good scholarship. I could refuse to go to Abbot and come home, but then I'd end up going to four different high schools. I'm actually glad when vacations end and I go back to Abbot. Poor Cookie is stuck listening to their constant bickering.

I come home and help whenever I get weekend leave. When the Franks, Mom and Dad's friends from the Philippines, came for a visit I heard them talking while I did the dishes. None of them get Social Security, because it was not deducted from their income while they worked abroad. Rules for employees working outside the U.S. are different. The companies they worked for were not required to pay the company's portion of Social Security, nor were they required to deduct the employees portion. At the time, the Franks and my folks did not understand the significance of not contributing to Social Security. The government thinks they're rich, because they own stocks, so they pay high taxes. Mr. Frank points out that it's a huge inequity for them, because none of them own a house that has gained in value for decades like the people here. Their pensions are small, so inflation is eating them alive. I used to want to grow up fast so I could be an adult, but this sounds awful.

Mother whines a lot with all of her "how I sacrifice" jazz. Dad never complains, he just stoically clams up. His limp has gotten worse, so they went to Boston to the Lahey Clinic to find out what's wrong with him and got bad news. Dad has the same degenerative spinal disease that his sister Annie had.

"He's got to stay on his feet," Mother insists. "The family had to support Annie for seven long years in a nursing home." Mom hates it when people get sick. Dad is older than she is. Maybe she's worried that he will have to go to a nursing home. Maybe she's worried that we'll be poor again the way we were when my real father died during the Depression.

Maine winters are the wrong type of weather for Dad. The cold exacerbates his spinal condition, but he is determined to make it work for the family. I don't fit in with these Portland Country Club and yacht club kids who have known each other all their lives. Cookie hasn't gotten close to any of the kids either. None of the kids from her junior high seem to live nearby.

All of us miss the resort where we used to spend our New York summers. After our first year in Portland, the resort owner sold us a little lot nearby so we could build a camp. This project, now underway, is picking up the family tempo. In spite of his limp, Dad cuts small trees and paints. He has a little shed in back of the house where he putters around building shelves for the living room and kitchen on his workbench. Mother would prefer cupboards, but maybe later. She fixes the meals and cooks delicious fish and casseroles. As often as possible, my mother plays golf with her old buddies, which seems to lift her spirits.

I help some, but this fall I'm going to Smith College, so I don't have much time. I'm afraid that building this camp is a big risk for them on top of sending me to college. To pitch in, I have a waitress job at the resort where I serve three meals a day, seven days a week. The nice people give good tips, but crabby ones are cheap, so I won't make as much as I'd like to, but at least it's a job. I'm glad to be contributing.

One morning Mother starts complaining as soon as I walk into the house after I had just served breakfast to the guests at the resort. "Tell him he has to do more. I've done enough." She's referring to my Dad who is doing the best he can given his condition.

"My feet are killing me," I reply as I take off my white gunboat work oxfords and put my feet up on the window seat.

"Tell him he's not leaving me enough money." She grabs her purse and the car keys. "Go tell him right now." She slams the screen door, jumps into the Buick and roars off.

I change out of my breakfast serving uniform and slip into my penny loafers. Dad is out behind the shed refinishing a second-hand dry sink.

'How was breakfast?" he asks. "Did they get their coffee fast enough?"'

"I did my best." I offer him a paper-napkin wrapped morsel. "I brought you a blueberry muffin."

He puts his brush into the turpentine can and sits down in the rusty metal chair he hasn't got around to painting yet. The turpentine smell seems to keep the mosquitoes away.

I take the plunge. "Mother just drove into town. She's loaded for bear again. She told me to tell you you're not leaving her enough money."

"I'm leaving her all I can." He throws the paper napkin at the trash can and misses. "My working days are over." He picks up a stone and tosses it into the woods. "You know, before we moved up here, I tried to get a job with the State Department in China." He scratches the

179

peeling paint on his chair. "They picked a young guy with no experience. He wanted to send the Chinese Beautyrest mattresses."

I observe the ants climb in and out of the anthill on the side of the ledge. I hate being in the middle like this. I don't know what to say.

Dad tries a joke to make me feel better. "There was another job in Southern India, but I didn't pursue it. I didn't want to send you to the University of Lahore."

I laugh, more at ease with Dad than I have ever been with Mom. High up in the pitch pine, the ever-present red squirrel scolds and drops bits of pinecone on our heads. I look up. "There he goes. He's so territorial."

"You know," Dad says. "I don't really know that much about her. I'm not even sure how old she is. She told me the town records burned. She never mentions her family."

Surprised by this sudden confidence, I look toward his still distinguished profile. "You're right. She never does."

"Sometimes I think she's keeping secrets. Sometimes I wonder what she knows herself." Figuring he has said too much, Dad pushes himself up from the rusty chair and limps toward the shed, his back round with defeat. My heart sinks at this sight.

I hate this. Dad might not be my real father, but he's my most real parent. I can tell he's in pain, but he never complains. Sometimes I hear Mother tell him, "It's up to you. I've done enough." I see that Dad wants the very best for both Cookie and me and he never expects anything back. I feel closer to him in this moment as he reveals the same feeling of isolation that I sense from the void of Mom's inner life. There is a piece missing. We both know it.

He does a smart thing one night before we leave for Smith. "You're only eighteen," he says. Legally you can't drink, but that won't matter in college. Here, try a Tom Collins."

It's delicious. It's fun. My face grows warm.

"Here." He fixes another.

Mellow. Sweet. This is the way to have fun at a party. After swilling the third drink, I get dizzy. Then I throw up.

"Okay," Dad says. "Now you know what liquor can do. Be careful. Don't ever go up to some fraternity guy's room and let him give you a drink."

It's a great warning. I'll never go all the way before I get married. What if I got pregnant? I'd have to figure out how to get an abortion, otherwise they'd throw me to the wolves for disgracing the family name. Still, who knows what they'd think if the guy was rich enough?

15. Romance and Reg

Mother is almost more excited than I am when we drive to Smith College. All summer she's been telling everyone, "Paula's going to Smith." I'm glad that she's actually proud. It's a major investment now that they're retired.

Mom and Dad look disgusted when we pull up to my dorm, Park House. It's a big square Victorian building that looks like it's probably next on the teardown list. Smith has small residence houses, not huge dorms. The gloomy mahogany woodwork bordering the walls is clearly a part of the venerable Smith tradition. It reminds me very much of Abbot. We sign in with the student sitting under the "welcome freshmen" sign.

Someone calls out, "Man on third," as we trudge up to my room with my suitcases and desk lamp.

"Good God. Pull-chain toilets," Dad says as we pass the bathroom.

Mother shakes her head. "Two thousand dollars a year for this?"

"Shh." Other students are looking at us. I lead the way to my room. Our beds are camp cots, but the walls are painted a cheery yellow.

Our vintage house soon feels like home. The food is so good that I'd be fat if the campus wasn't so large. I have to hoof it across campus several times a day. I discover that Smith is full of superstars and rich girls rattling on about their coming debuts. Some will "come out" on their own. The lesser ones will join a group at the Waldorf Astoria in Manhattan. Characters abound here. One Southern girl from a plantation brought her horse. Another is a model who has graced the cover of *The Ladies' Home Journal*. They all seem to have trust funds. If they don't, they were at least valedictorians of their high school classes. I'm doing all I can just focusing on passing the term.

Dad told me to take chemistry. "It's the key to the future," he said.

I fail the first midterm, which is a shock. I'm doing okay in freshman English and French III, but Survey of European History is a killer. We seem to cover a century a day. Here I am with the cream of the crop and I can't help wondering why they accepted me.

We wear Bermuda shorts and knee socks, even when it's cold, but just like at Abbot, skirts are required at dinner. Afterwards, we have coffee and conversation in the housemother's living room. Most of the girls chat away with ease, but a few look like they'd rather be reading like I would. Classes run six days a week and students can only leave after Saturday morning classes. Some girls meet their dates under the clock at the Biltmore Hotel in New York. It sounds so romantic.

We have to sign in at the house at 10:15 p.m. on weekdays, midnight on Fridays and Sundays, but on Saturday nights we can stay out until 1:00 a.m. The rules are fine with me, since I don't have a boyfriend. If I'm trying to fend off some blind date before curfew, I go smoke a cigarette in the car or on the porch.

Not everyone is as prudish as I am. Kimmy, a girl in my house, is leaving after this semester, because she's pregnant. She got married just before her husband left for Korea. They're allowing her to finish the term in Park House, but only because her roommate, Pam, got written permission from her parents allowing Pam to room with a married woman. The old double standard. They've decided Kimmy's husband is old enough to fight and die for us, while we are treated like overprotected children.

———

Money is getting even tighter at home. Mother has budgeted a $40 a month allowance, which I appreciate, but it's not enough. More worrisome is when she sometimes forgets to enclose the check. I feel bad asking her for it. She sends a letter faithfully every week and wants one back with all the details of my life. I get the feeling that she's living vicariously through me. She has tried so hard to provide me with the kind of childhood she would have liked. I wonder if she's ashamed of her background. That would explain why she won't talk about it. I wish I'd been smart enough to get a scholarship, so my poor parents wouldn't have to foot the entire bill. The scholarship girls live in their own houses. There they can prepare their own food and do their own cleaning. I think I would like that kind of independence.

Smith is intimidating. Sometimes I still wonder why I'm here. Everyone here is so gorgeous, so rich, so articulate, and most of all, so smart. The school blazer gives you an identity. I never got a navy blue blazer with the official Abbot seal when I attended there. I didn't dare ask for the money. Cookie is going to Abbot too, so I told her to get the blazer. It will give her confidence and besides she got a great scholarship, so I figure she's earned it. At Smith I wear the usual uniform of Bermudas, knee socks, and a button-down shirt with a sweater. But the gray flannel of my Bermudas isn't thick enough, my shirts aren't Brooks Brothers, and my sweaters aren't cashmere. I try to make it not matter, but I can feel the other girls' judgmental glances.

With Christmas vacation coming up, my debutante classmates are focusing on their coming debuts. I've been invited to the Dubutante Ball at Yale. It's in the middle of vacation. I guess they got my name from the freshman handbook and figured I'm not a "deb," since I'm from Maine. I've decided not to go. It'll cost too much. I'd have to take the train to New Haven and stay overnight somewhere. I've been through enough of these dumb freshman mixers trying to make small talk and besides, everyone will be drinking too much.

———

Life takes off after Christmas, thanks to my roommate, Zizi, who is dating a fellow named Harry at Williams, one of the small, so-called "potted ivy-league" colleges in Williamstown, Massachusetts. In

February, they bring me along with them to the Williams Winter Carnival with Zonker, Harry's roommate.

We make the rounds of the ice sculptures and drink a brew here and there — only Zonker quaffs a few too many and passes out on the grungy couch in the Psi U frat house. By then it's late. Zizi and Harry have disappeared, so I decide to hitch a ride back to the rooming house where Zizi and I are staying. I stand in the doorway of the Psi U house in my high heels and gird myself for a slog through the snow to the parking lot.

Behind me a low rumbling voice asks, "May I carry you?" I turn and see a tall, broad-shouldered guy with an uneven face and a squashed-in nose like a prizefighter looming over me. Not a pretty boy -- but a dangerously appealing one. I sense his rippling muscles under his black varsity letter sweater with the purple W. He doesn't wait for an answer, but swoops me up in his arms, carries me across the parking lot, and deposits me beside the car. When I thank him, he says, "'Tis a pleasure with a load so light." His close-cropped curly hair is black and the way he slides his tongue inside his cheek makes me sorry he's put me down.

Bowing slightly, he introduces himself. "Preston."

"Hi Preston, I'm Paula."

"Where are you from, Paula?"

"Smith."

"Oh? What house?"

"Park." I'm thinking in monosyllables.

"No kidding." His smile broadens. "Do you know Stephanie Trowbridge?"

I rack my brain until I realize that I do. "Sort of, she's a junior, isn't she?"

"She's from my home town. Georgetown."

Everyone is piling into the car for the ride to the rooming house. I perch on the edge of the back seat and wave as we pull away. Preston waves back. Huge wet snowflakes settle on his curly hair.

That is the beginning. Two weeks later, Preston drives over the Mohawk Trail, picks me up at Park House, and takes me to Rahars, the downtown bar where they never card Smith girls. He has this habit of never saying "yes" or "no." Instead he rumbles, "affirmative" or "negative," so when we're together his bass voice has me quivering like a fiddle string.

Nothing else matters now that I've met Preston. I'm in love. Spring has brought a round of fraternity parties and picnics, touch football and dances. Back and forth I go in Preston's black convertible over the hairpin turns on the Mohawk Trail, feeling like a princess every weekend for the rest of the term.

———

There's a sour note at home. I end the year on "Reg" — The Registrar's list of students on academic probation. With better grades I might have been able to transfer to one of the co-op scholarship houses where I could earn my keep. I know the tuition is killing my parents; Dad's pension is small, and Mother pays for so much already. Oh, they haven't told me to drop out in so many words, but Dad keeps pushing the idea of Katherine Gibbs Secretarial School where I'd learn some practical skills so I could work up to being a crack secretary. Mother wants a detailed rundown on any boy I go out with. Not only the guy -- but also his entire family. Last fall I spent a couple of weekends at Harvard and MIT. She thought I should have been more impressed with those guys. I haven't told her much about Preston. We write lots of letters, but I don't really know that much about him. I know he's rich, but I don't tell Mother that he went to Ann Rockefeller's coming out party.

Preston visits us in Maine right after freshman year. It turns out to be sort of tense. Dad won't talk while Mother fawns all over him, asking if he knows any of their China friends around Washington. He doesn't.

"My mother lives in Georgetown. She spends a lot of time with Fostie Dulles," he explains. Fostie just happens to be John Foster Dulles, President Eisenhower's Secretary of State. Mom is, of course, impressed albeit a bit nervous.

I begin to notice that our house looks bare. All the Chinese stuff is packed in boxes, because they've sold the place. Mother tells Preston about six times that we're going to spend the summer at the cottage. To escape, I ask Preston if he'd like to drive up to the cottage for the day.

"I'm not driving another hundred miles just to see some damn cottage," he snaps.

This is not like college. Our backgrounds are totally different. Preston purses his lips. His belly laugh is gone. All he says is "yes," or "no" when my mother asks him questions.

After he leaves, Mother gushes, "He has such wonderful manners. He made his bed every morning."

I think they were intimidated.

So, we're all spending the summer at the cottage we love. This winter, they're going to Florida and Cookie's going to Abbot. I'm happy for her and Mom and Dad are relieved that she has a handsome scholarship.

Mother and Dad have put their worldly goods in storage. They're eager to try Florida this winter, but it's dawning on them that Florida won't work, because Maine summers are too short for them to spend half the year in the cottage.

I carry in firewood for the antique black stove with naked cherubs gamboling on the door, but that stove produces more smoke than heat. My parents will stay at the cottage through October, then leave before the pipes freeze. They have bought the lot across the street from the house they just sold, with plans to build another place when they get back from Florida next spring.

After another summer of waitressing, I land the job of Park House pot washer in September. I disappear into the kitchen after dinner to scrub the fixin's for sixty student dinners. I haven't told my parents or Preston, and I doubt that my housemates have noticed. At least now I don't have to beg Mother for the money she can't afford to send me. After I do the pots, I retire to the smoking room and chain smoke all evening over my piles of reading.

Preston and I are hot and heavy. I spend every waking moment thinking about him. Zizi calls him the sex symbol, and that he is. My hunk of a boyfriend fills a room when he walks in and heads turn. I'm having the time of my life as we go to all the Williams football games. This year they've held a contest to choose a name for their mascot, the purple cow. At the end of football season, they announce the winner: "Ephelia."

We have many torrid sessions in the front seat of his black convertible and in his room at the Psi U house, but we never go all the way. One night he shows me the condom his father gave him. "In case I ever need it," he says solemnly. But we always stop in time. What if I got pregnant?

When we aren't making out, Preston runs me down the way my mother does. Sometimes he makes me feel like I'm some barefoot hillbilly who lives in a house with a dirt floor. I criticize him back, but I'm not sure it's such a good idea. I feel like Mother with her, "I'm only telling you what's wrong with you for your own good so you can improve yourself" routine. I exorcise my feelings by writing him letters, but I begin to think I should hold my letters for a day before I send them. Feelings get hurt.

One week I embarrassed Preston when we played touch football with his fraternity brothers. I'm not sure why, but I think it was the way I was dressed. This was particularly hurtful, because that weekend I wore my Shetland sweater and the matching tweed skirt I had made. I've learned to sew after all those visits watching Aunt Alice. At least she appreciates my efforts. I knit the sweater too. Mother says my knitting drives her nuts. I mostly do it to cut down on my smoking. I thought it was a sharp-looking outfit, but Preston may not have been of the same opinion. He is so rich, he gets a haircut every week, and the cloth of his gray flannel pants is so thick it could stand alone. Sometimes he tells me that I don't fit his concept of the ideal woman, whatever that is. It's certainly not his mother. She's on her third husband. As a child, Preston went to a psychiatrist, because he hated her.

By Thanksgiving our love affair ends with a crash. Preston is quiet one Sunday as he drives me back to Smith along the twisting Mohawk Trail after a weekend of partying at the Psi U house. After our usual steamy session in the front seat, he reaches into the back seat, grabs a paper bag, and pulls out a purple and gold striped Williams scarf for me. Here is the preamble I've been waiting for. The prelude to the letter sweater, the fraternity pin, and eventually, the engagement ring. Instead, Preston tells me that we're through. "It's just that I have this image in mind of my ideal woman, and you don't make the grade," he says offhandedly. He's timed it well. The girl on watch inside Park House is blinking the porch lights. The witching hour has arrived, and we have five minutes to get inside. "But please call on me if you ever need anything," he says, reaching across the seat to open my door.

I run up the stairs to my room, holding the scarf across my face to hide my tears. The scarf smells like Preston. I take it to bed and inhale it all night long.

I mope in the library. I study all the time, but I don't get off probation. I wear my snazzy purple and gold scarf wherever I go so people will *think* I have a boyfriend at Williams. Nothing matters. A midwinter blizzard buries my bike somewhere on campus. So what? It'll turn up in the spring. I drag to the library carrying all my textbooks. My arms are sore, but I can't concentrate. I sneak envious glances at girls sporting fraternity pins or letters on their oversized black sweaters; A for Amherst, B for Brown, D for Dartmouth, H for Harvard, P for Princeton, W for Williams Y for Yale. I've lost my chance for a W. I have to go back to the beginning and start all over again.

I'm a greasy grind. I never smile. I never ask for help. I never go to professors' office hours, because I'm too embarrassed to be failing their courses. I continue to wash pots. Mother continues to forget to enclose checks in her letters.

"Why not try Katherine Gibbs?" my parents ask. Another alternative is Scripps College in Southern California. They offer a scholarship for a graduate of a New England secondary school. My parents now yearn for California. Their reasons multiply each time I go home to visit. Maine is too cold. Dad might slip on the ice. The neighbors are frumpy. Since they made a profit on their first house, they might also do well on the one they've built across the street. I must admit, the reasoning makes sense. California might be the answer.

At the end of the year I finally get off probation. My parents are not impressed and they offer me the choice of Scripps College or Katherine Gibbs. I choose Scripps, because it is a college. I'm not sure why I want to stay in college. Perhaps I realize going out to work means that you're an adult and I'm not quite ready to be an adult.

16. Out West and Back East

I break up the cross-country train trip with a visit to Aunt Alice who now lives in Oklahoma. Her round and cheerful form stands out in the platform crowd as the train pulls into the station. Beside her, my cousin Diane reaches for my suitcase as I step off the train.

"Look at you!" I give Diane a hug. "You're a full-fledged teenager."

"Yes," Diane brushes her bangs. "You have to drop me off at cheerleading practice on your way home," she grins. She's wearing a swirly little skirt and a top that shows off her new curves. My little cousin is not so little anymore.

Alice's home on a tree-lined street could be anywhere, except that it sits on a lot that is smaller than any I've noticed in New England. In spite of the vast western spaces surrounding us, these houses have little breathing room. We enter into what would have been the living room, except that it is Alice's workroom with bolts of fabric stacked in one corner, curtain rods and valances in another.

"Wow. You've branched out into your own drapery business Aunt Alice!"

"Yes. In Oklahoma I call myself a decorator. Since I've lived in New England, they think I'm old money," she winks.

I point to the rods and valances.

"After I make the draperies, Jim hangs them." Her husband Jim has retired from the Navy.

I settle into the guest room. Dropping my suitcase on the rug, I slip off my skirt and penny loafers. After two nights on the train jerking along the tracks on a straight-backed, wicker coach seat that sagged in the middle, my back is screaming. My neck pulls. I can't get to sleep, so I fill the tub and soak my weary bones. Too tired to shampoo my hair in the shower, I lather it, slide the length of the tub on my back, and rinse my hair by allowing it to float like seaweed.

"I didn't realize you had such a thriving business," I tell Alice the next morning. "No wonder you can't visit us in Maine."

"It's hard to get away. Your mother keeps inviting me." She looks out the window as a passing dog marks her tree. "Well ... you know ... your mother has been so good to me. She brought me to the U.S. from Canada when you were a baby." She pauses. "But something is always wrong with me. My clothes are flamboyant. My earrings dangle."

"Don't take it personally," I say. "Something is always wrong with me too."

She turns the bacon and whips the eggs with a whisk. "I know that Everett, your stepdad, looks down on me. He gets all dressed up in a suit and tie every day just to sit there and criticize everybody. Diane is afraid of him. She calls him Uncle Bushy Brows." I ponder how differently Diane and Aunt Alice perceive Everett's ways compared to the way he makes me feel special. Perceptions and misconceptions are so subjective.

For the rest of the morning my sweet aunt cuts fabric. We go to lunch at a lady's tearoom where the hostess seats us at a corner table surrounded by Mexican urns overflowing with drooping ferns. When our turkey club sandwiches and sweet tea arrive, she raises her glass in a toast. "You've grown into a beautiful young lady. Do you have a special boyfriend?"

"I did, but he dumped me." I grind my cigarette butt in the alabaster seashell ashtray. "I wasn't rich enough."

"Rich enough? Well, what about your father's money?"

"My father's money!" What on earth? Alice has always leveled with me. I repeat the story. "My father was a struggling young architect who got run down by a car in the Depression and left Mother penniless with me to raise."

Reaching across the table to squeeze my arm, Alice's voice shakes. "Baloney. Your father was a very wealthy man. He adored you. You were his only child. Why, everyone in the family knows you're an heiress."

A thought — who *are* these people in this family? -- flashes through my mind before I swallow and respond, "I guess everyone in the family but me knows. First I've ever heard of it." My voice shakes too. Mother might have money, but everyone in the family knew I was an heiress? Why the hell had I always felt it was my job to sweep the cinders?

"I don't know what's wrong with your mother," Alice says.

"Well, you know, they've spent so much money on our educations. Maybe it's gone by now. Cookie and I have always gone to excellent schools."

"Maybe so," Alice says. "Let's have baklavas for dessert," she tells the waitress who stands between the drooping ferns.

She says no more. Trying to absorb her news, I don't ask her. She's my mother's sister. They've shared more together than I will ever know. Once, on an earlier visit, I'd asked her what she knew about my father.

"Not much," she'd said. "They brought me for a visit before you were born. Your mother was his nurse. He seemed pretty old. But I was only nineteen, and most adults seemed old. Forty, sixty, seventy, they were all the same to me." I'd never mentioned her comments to Mother. I'd filed the information in the back of my mind along with all the other discrepancies about my real father Hans Pederson.

That evening, I get back on the train for my final sit-up-all-night-ride west in a car with more comfortable seats this time. In the morning, dusty mountains rise before me as we arrive in Claremont, California. Carrie, my designated "big sister" greets my train and drives me to Scripps in her convertible. There are flowers everywhere and Moorish type architecture. It's not Spain. It's Southern California where Spanish influenced architecture and Mexican food abounds.

"They call it the college in a garden," Carrie tells me, as she carries one of my suitcases along the eucalyptus-lined walkway to our dorm.

It's lovely, but I don't feel I belong here. I never wanted to leave New York and I never wanted to leave New England, and I never wanted to leave Smith, in spite of the misery of my sophomore year. Scripps is beautiful, but I feel unmoored at these beer parties in the orange groves with girls who slather on cake makeup in the bright sunlight and boys who wear Balboa Blue pants instead of khakis. I went to three high schools and I don't want to go to two colleges. I don't want to be an expat like my parents, eternally casting my net somewhere else. I want roots. Besides, Preston will soon get his Navy discharge. On the East Coast, I might see him again.

I write cheery letters home as long as I can, then I write one that tells the truth.

"The time has come to tell you that I don't like it here. I really want to go back and finish my senior year at Smith."

Reluctantly my parents agree. It's a selfish decision, and my parents are going along with it out of love for me. They really do sacrifice for me, and now they want me to be happy even though I'm lousing up their move to California. But who knows? They complain so much that I wonder if they'd like it any better out here.

By the time I get home, they've sold the second house -- the one they built across the street from the first house. They've decided to try Florida again. If that doesn't work, they'll rent an apartment in downtown Portland. Mother claims that Dad doesn't want to own any property, but I know that it's really because icy walks and snow-covered driveways are no good for a man who can barely walk. He's graduating from using a cane to needing a walker. Mother is embarrassed to be seen with him.

"I married him to take care of me," she wails, "but now I have to take care of him."

For the second time she had married a successful older man beyond his prime, then blamed him for getting old. Dad never complained, but his hurt silences lengthened as his health, his marriage, and his A-1 status diminished.

Still, we had the little cottage, our sanctuary, down the dirt road in the place that was one constant in our lives. Once we helped Dad up the porch steps, he was able to navigate the hall between the living, dining, and bedroom areas, holding on to the back of the couch and the bureaus for support. Each morning he would appear at breakfast clean shaven, dressed in a freshly laundered white shirt, suit and tie. Although he lived to be ninety-two and could barely walk, for breakfast he loved apple pie with cheddar cheese, or doughnuts -- the old fashioned kind that sink like lead in your stomach, not the modern kind that feel like you're biting into a pillow.

After breakfast he would drag himself to the couch and extend his legs, revealing his black socks, tightened by his swollen ankles, below the cuffs of his pants. "Doris," he'd bark, "Get me the *Today Show*. Channel Thirteen."

Mother would charge in from the kitchen, wiping her hands on her apron, muttering, "For God's sake." She rarely watched TV. She was always working: baking, sweeping, raking. I'd bring friends home to try and cheer them up. Nothing worked. Still, she played occasional golf and invited friends for bridge.

"Nobody asks us back because Dad can't walk," she'd complain.

I often wish that Dad had lived long enough to have a remote for his TV and a motorized wheelchair.

———

Senior year at Smith I get back on probation. I have an awful time with my comprehensive English exam. Just one provocative quote followed by the word "Discuss." We're supposed to discuss it for three hours. I look at the floor as I hand my blue book to Mr. Hill, the English Department chair.

He calls me to his office the following week. I cross the campus with azaleas, quince and tulips in bloom everywhere. Sunbathing students lounge on blankets, Bermuda shorts rolled high only to be quickly lowered as student grass cops come into view, ready to enforce the tanning rules. The college handbook prescribes the allowable length of bare leg and the permitted $45°$ seating angle. No sunbathing for me. I slump as I enter Mr. Hill's office. I must have failed. Now I won't graduate. Maybe I can blame it on my junior year at another school.

He motions me to a chair across from his desk. His pate is shiny, his eyes watery and pale. He opens my blue book and tells me, "You have excellent insights, but you're so disorganized. If only you'd come to the Freshman Written English Clinic."

Such a thought had never occurred to me. All through college I've been so worried about wearing the wrong clothes, spending my

201

parents' money, and breaking up with Preston, that I've hidden at the back of classrooms, mortified at my stupidity. Turns out I'm not stupid after all. I will graduate. At the bottom of my class, to be sure, but now I can go forward with confidence to — what? I'll figure that out after one more summer of waitressing at the resort. I should at least be able to save enough for a security deposit on an apartment somewhere.

Graduation brings a round of speakers and family receptions. Adlai Stevenson is our commencement speaker -- a year before he makes his second unsuccessful run for the presidency against Dwight Eisenhower. As the father of three boys, he states, he is uncertain how to address "several hundred young, charming, feminine eggheads." He advises us to guide our families from the hearth. For the rest of our lives we've remembered one stirring sentence:

"I want merely to tell you young ladies that I think there is much you can do about that [nuclear proliferation] crisis in the humble role of housewife -- which statistically, is what most of you are going to be whether you like the idea or not just now -- and you'll like it!"

I liked it, but not all of us did. Gloria Steinem graduated in 1956, a year later. A leader in the thick of the feminist movement, she founded *Ms.* magazine. Nine years later, my classmate, the renowned poet Sylvia Plath, took her little children to her neighbor's, came back home, and laid her head inside her gas oven.

We attend several gala receptions. Out of their comfort zone, my parents hover uneasily on the fringes. I wish I could protect them. I've learned to navigate the varied collegiate social strata, but they feel the way I did as a freshman. Everyone else seems rich and successful. Bent over his cane, Dad drags his bum leg from one event to another. Mother, embarrassed by her crippled older husband, laughs nervously and fawns at other parents. I want to tell them to relax and enjoy the commencement. These are fine people -- A-1 people who work hard to make a better world. They are healers, teachers, visionaries who create jobs, philanthropists who support worthy causes.

Driving back to Maine, in a rare stab at communication, I thank my parents for being so good to me. "You sent me to fine schools. You straightened my teeth. We've lived in New York and Maine. I hope that I can repay your efforts by making you proud of me."

Dad stares silently ahead. Mother purses her lips and nods. Maybe they think they have wasted their money since I'm not engaged.

17. My Own Life

It's time for me to leave home and find a real job. My roommate Zizi's fiancé is a divinity student in Boston. Preston, out of the Navy, is entering Harvard Law School. Our romance could be on again, so I head for Boston. Zizi and I find a postage-stamp apartment, the upstairs of a little Cambridge house near Harvard Square.

I'm delighted to land a job as an assistant secretary at Harvard College at a salary of $200 a month. It's 1955 and our monthly rent is $70 — $35 apiece, so Zizi and I can get by on our starvation salaries. We chip in $5 a week for food to carry us through to the weekend when we hope someone will provide us with dinner. I walk to work, passing Harvard's museum of glass flowers along the way. Miraculously, I have enough money left to shop at Peck & Peck. I buy a black princess-style overcoat that fits my seventeen-inch waist. The memory of Preston's snide remarks about my sweaters prompts me to buy a couple of cashmere sweaters. I develop an eye for classy bargains at Filene's basement.

Cookie goes to Cornell — with a Teagle scholarship since she's a Standard Oil daughter. I probably would have gone there too if we'd known about the scholarship in time. Not only does Cookie become a reporter for the *Cornell Daily Sun*, she dates an editor. Our parents give him a frosty reception when he visits one weekend in Maine.

"They'll never be happy unless I marry the son of the President of General Motors," Cookie says.

I try to console her, "Rich boys make our parents nervous. Remember how it was with Preston?"

Eventually, Cookie rates approval when she is elected to Phi Beta Kappa, and again when she graduates and lands a job as secretary to the president of a Connecticut corporation. "Why, she even rode to the airport with him in the company limousine while he gave her dictation," Dad says. His comment blows right past me. They are constantly comparing us with each other.

My rekindled romance with Preston soon grinds to a mutual halt. We've both outgrown our need for advice on how to improve ourselves for our own good. As for my job, since I graduated at the bottom of my college class, I find myself awed by the brilliance of Harvard students, grads, and faculty. Depressed once again, it takes me until I am thirty to realize that I'm not stupid and that hard work, common sense, and resourcefulness will carry me through.

The Fallons, China friends of my parents, invite me to dinner where I meet Chip, a first year student at Harvard Business School, and the son of another Standard Oil man who lived in China. We call the Fallons "the go-betweens," because of their effort to set us up in a

Chinese-style arranged marriage. I stroll over the Charles River Bridge to the "B School" — as HBS is called — for visits with Chip. Due to his tough schedule, we have a low-key courtship. First-year students are assigned big papers due every other Saturday night at nine.

Chip never tells me what is wrong with me for my own good. He never tells me I don't measure up to his concept of the ideal woman. He likes me the way I am. We seem to be idealists in a materialistic age. The medical and law students I date are focused on their coming lucrative practices. In contrast, Chip, supposedly training to be a money grubbing capitalist, refreshingly lays out his hope for world peace, "If people will learn to trade together, there will be no more war." I like that. He's thoughtful.

Shortly before the spring term ends, we head out to the countryside for a picnic. Parking by the side of the road, we walk through a field of wildflowers, stopping at a stone wall, a few boulders spilling off the top as it curves. Chip spreads a blanket and pats the spot beside him as he kneels.

"Here. I want to read you something." He pulls some papers out of a manila envelope. "It's one of my cases; I'd like your ideas." He reads the first two pages — a case about diamond engagement rings. "These cases go on forever. You get my drift. What's a good ad? A good tag line?" He stretches out and leans on his elbow. "Your kisses sparkle more than any diamond? You're brighter than a diamond?"

"I like them both." I lie back and cradle my head on my palms.

The warmth of sunlight bathes us. The drone of bees surrounds us. The songs of birds delight us.

207

"Oh hell! I'll never be an ad man, but I want to spend my life with you. Will you marry me?"

"Well of course. You are absolutely the right man for me." We roll to the center of the blanket.

Paula's engagement photo 1956, age 23.

He's the right man for Dad too. Dad knew Chip's father in China. "I never heard a bad word about Fred Abbott," he says.

Mother is more ambivalent. She wants me to come back to Portland and join the Junior League. "You won't marry a Portland boy just to spite me," she says in a fit of pique. I'm dumbfounded. What can she say against Chip, a graduate of Exeter, Amherst, and the Harvard Business School?

I register my gift preferences at Shreve, Crump & Lowe, the Boston equivalent of Tiffany's, as I plan the life that both Mother and the bridal magazines suggest lies ahead. Royal Doulton china, Chantilly sterling. I acquire a trousseau with some vague idea of living in a large, suburban home where I'll spend my days attending meetings at art museums and historical societies. At the same time, I look forward to my escape from the confident and competitive people to whom I still feel so inferior.

Planning the wedding is a high stress event for my parents. They'll have to entertain old China hands Dad hasn't seen for years. Mother wants an Episcopal service at the fashionable stone church near our former Portland homes. I opt for a simple ceremony in the old Congregational meetinghouse on a hill near our cottage. As I dress for the wedding, Mother helps me adjust my veil. She stands back and cocks her head. Then she leans forward and clears her throat before she whispers her one and only comment to me about the birds and bees. "It helps if you put a pillow under your hips." I feel pain bleeding through her comment. Somewhere along the line she's been hurt.

Poor Dad. By now he can barely walk. Ever focused on looking his best, he has to stagger down the aisle beside me in front of all those people. Resplendent in a hoop-skirted, lace-covered gown borrowed from one of their A-1 friends, I carry my daisy bouquet in my right hand, while my left firmly supports Dad's arm as I try to keep him from falling.

The afternoon reception is held in the resort's all-purpose hall used for movies, square dances, and bingo games. Our friends have decorated the building with big white paper wedding bells and streamers. We've sent Chip's New York ushers out in the woods to cut pine trees and boughs that fill the church and the pine-paneled reception hall with woodsy fragrance.

The buffet table holds a bowl of rum punch with a ladle, and little glass cups. All along Dad's been saying, "I'll decide between champagne and rum punch when we get to the liquor store."

"I'll take a dozen bottles of rum," he tells the clerk when we pick up the booze.

"Rum punch'll be terrific," I say.

Plates of finger sandwiches flank the sides of the punch bowl. After the toast and the cutting of the cake, Chip and I make the rounds. Leona, a Standard Oil widow, pats the chair beside her, inviting me to sit. Well fortified with rum punch, she begins to reminisce.

"I was in China all those many years ago with your parents — or at least with your father and his first wife, Harriet." She drums her fingers on the table. "Harriet absolutely hated China."

"Oh?" I have never heard of Harriet.

Leona inspects a ridge on her fingernail polish. "Of course, all of us put up with the missionary medical care. Actually, it was quite good. We never understood why Harriet carried on so. After all, she was a Christian Scientist."

Twirling a sapphire ring on her right hand, Leona doesn't notice my breathing tighten. "Harriet refused to come back to China after your father's home leave. We felt so sorry for your father. He left the company." She frowns. "I forgot where he went."

"He went to work for STANCO, a subsidiary."

Leona looks up at a paper wedding bell, off on a reverie of the triumphs and tribulations of her Far Eastern years. Remembering that I am there, she turns to me. "We were so glad when he married your mother — such a beautiful young heiress. You're just as pretty as she is."

I stand. The sides of my hoop skirt squash into an oval as I run my palms down my hips. "Leona, I'm so glad you've come. I hope you're finding many old friends here." Suddenly dizzy, I set one foot in front of the other and move on to the next table, trying to shove this bombshell to the back of my mind. Maybe I've had too much rum punch myself. Leona has just told me that *both* of my parents are frauds. Oh, I'm used to Mother's waffling, her tirades on the rare occasions that the subject of my real father comes up. By now I've determined that he was no pauper. I figure she wants to spare me the nature of his crimes to protect me. But Dad! He too has a secret past.

A salty breeze wafts in from the bay accompanied by the sounds of flapping sails and distant motors. This is my wedding day. Look at this nice reception my parents are putting on. It's not easy for them. Everyone is having a good time. Mother is animated and absolutely beautiful. Dad is finally relaxing, laughing as he visits with these old friends that he never would have seen again unless I was marrying Chip. I'll deal with this later.

"You're awfully quiet," Chip says as we drive up the coast to Boothbay Harbor after we've raced down the all-purpose-hall ramp, dodging handfuls of rice. My Uncle George has reserved a whiz-bang of a room for us at the Village Inn where he worked as a desk clerk after he retired from the Merchant Marine.

I tell Chip the story during dinner. I'm not hungry. "They have all these secrets," I say. "It knocks me for a loop when I find out. Mother goes to pieces when I ask."

"Maybe they're hiding their pasts from you because they're ashamed," Chip says. "Maybe they want to protect you."

At the inn, I take a long soak in the bathtub before I don my white nightgown.

"They should have told you," Chip says, gently rubbing my back. "This was no way to find out."

"I feel like I'm walking on quicksand," I say. "All three of my parents are mysteries."

He slides into bed beside me. I slide off my nightgown. I forget about my three parents as we begin our married life.

———

We settle into corporate life with the Corning Glass Works in upstate New York. Instead of joining country clubs, we have babies — four in five and a half years. We're so busy that many of the momentous events of the sixties slide right past us — the Vietnam War, the Beatles. We never even buy a TV until the fall of 1963 — just in time to sit weeping before the screen as little John-John Kennedy salutes the flag when his father's casket passes by on the caisson with the riderless horse.

The sixties are a time of frequent corporate transfers. IBM employees joke that the company acronym stands for "I've Been Moved." We spend only a year in Corning before our first transfer. In Bradford, a rural town in northern Pennsylvania, we find a Salvation-Army type store where we buy a secondhand crib for our daughter, Beth, and thirteen months later, a second one for our son, Jeffrey. Because we will someday inherit our parents' "priceless" Chinese antiques, we figure that this is a time to live frugally and learn new skills as we plan for our future. Since Aunt Alice taught me to sew during my childhood visits to her, I make my own maternity clothes along with floor-to-ceiling drapes for the living-room picture window. Other new skills include cooking and canning vegetables from the productive garden Chip plants on the site of a former barn.

Mother bravely comes to help when both Beth and Jeffrey are born and a year later when I have a tonsillectomy after running a low-grade fever for nearly a year. She shops, cooks, gardens, and irons Chip's button-down shirts. My mother knows all about babies. Like any helpful grandmother, she gets up in the middle of the night to change diapers and bring me the babies to nurse.

"What they say is true," I tell her. "You never appreciate your parents until you have your own children." Proudly I show her the strawberry jam I've made from the berries I've picked, as well as the jars of tomatoes I've canned.

It seems that time and distance have mellowed her. Mom is ready to accept my life as I am living it. She smiles patiently. But she is so tired that we never ask her to help again. Now in his mid-seventies, Dad is frail. He needs her at his side.

They return to spend Christmas with us the following year, on their way to Florida where they plan yet again to search for a winter home. As we gather 'round the tree on Christmas morning, Mother presents me with a huge silver box wrapped with an outsized silver bow. I gasp, as expected, open the box, and lift out a silver fox jacket.

"Ohhh, how magnificent!" I try to glow with appreciation, but my mind goes back to that Christmas when I was twelve. This is the bride doll redux.

"Thank you *so* much!" I exclaim, hand on my heart. Inwardly I seethe. Hasn't she noticed the way we live? If only she'd given me a few months of diaper service to help when the new baby arrives in another month.

Three-year-old Beth cradles Chatty Cathy, her gift from Santa. She rocks her back and forth and pulls the string on her back to make her talk. Two-year-old Jeff fills his dump truck with farm animals from his Old MacDonald set.

Suddenly Mother begins to weep. She buries her face in her hands. "You should be out dancing," she chokes between heaving sobs.

Beth grabs Chatty Cathy and runs to the bathroom. Jeff shoves his dump truck toward the kitchen. It hits the wall and sends the farm animals flying as it tips.

A scream comes from the bathroom. I run to Beth. "What's wrong?"

"Chatty Cathy told me to give her a bath," she wails. "Now she won't talk to me." Beth had destroyed Chatty Cathy's voice box when she set her in a sink full of water.

After I coax everyone back to the tree, Dad peers at me over his glasses. Nobody speaks. What is there to say? Mother's meaning is clear. She's given me the silver fox jacket, because she's had a brief fantasy that this is her last chance to help me lead the life she's imagined for me. Dad probably feels the same way, but he has the sense to keep quiet. After all their hard work and sacrifice, we have failed to become A-1 people. Instead we've turned into breeders and farmers who live in the sticks.

PART III
THEIR LIVES 1864 – 1933

18. Huchulaks, Huculaks, Hushlaks

In 2008, nine years after Mother's death, I open an envelope with a Vancouver, B.C. postmark. Genevieve Huchulak, who is evidently my first cousin, plans to host a family reunion in Alberta the following summer. Genevieve, a music and French teacher in Vancouver, includes a color-coded database in her reunion material that names six branches of the Huchulak, Huculak, and Hushlak family as the spelling of the family name has evolved through the years. Mother had once mentioned the name of her family, Hushlak, but then quickly moved on to claim that the waspy name of Pederson had always been hers. Genevieve's database indicates that including spouses, I have more than fifty first cousins.

As the reunion planning proceeds, I learn that four of the six branches plan to send members; one cousin will fly from London, another from Toronto. Fifty people, in fact, plan to attend. What a gift my cousin Genevieve is handing me. Perhaps meeting my family will clear up the mystery that still surrounds my mother, my stepfather, my real father, and me. Maybe this reunion will clear up the lifelong mystery of my heritage.

Forty-four years earlier, in 1964, I had taken Mother to see the movie, *Dr. Zhivago*, when I lived in Greensboro. Barely into the story, she had suddenly gasped and clapped her face with her hand as the camera moved from the vast panorama of the Russian winter into a bare room, where a small child stood in a circle of somber adults in dark coats. They watched as a man nailed a wooden coffin shut.

"What's wrong?" I had asked.

"Nothing," she'd whispered, pushing her knuckles against her teeth. "It reminds me of my childhood."

But I felt that she had become that child -- alone and unprotected in the circle of grownups. Someone important to her had died. I felt her terror as we observed the grim expressions on the faces of the adults staring down at that child. Mother's "nothing" was a great big something that had slipped past her guard.

It had taken me years to understand that beneath her controlling veneer of sophistication and glamour, she was a deeply private, shy, and often frightened person. Instead of exposing her wounds, she'd tell me about the healthy lifestyle shared with her siblings growing up on their Alberta farm. My mom had excellent teeth. There were no soft drinks. Cottage cheese and vegetables came from the root cellar. She'd played with Helen and Alice, her two younger sisters and her younger brother Alec, in their horse-drawn sleigh in the snow. Violin music made her sad, because her father, a cheerful man who told his children stories, played the violin. I don't recall any mention of her mother, but somehow I knew that her mom's life centered on the Orthodox Church.

Mother's sister Alice had also never mentioned their family during my visits to her home. What I had come to realize was that my fancy schooling had shaped me into somebody they were not. Both of them worried about what I would think if I learned of their peasant origins. Mother also felt obliged to hide her first marriage to a man, who although old enough to be her grandfather, had still managed to sire me.

———

Of course I'll go to the reunion. Our daughters Beth and Wendy, and Wendy's husband Matt, plan to come too. We'll be the only U.S. relatives there. Cookie and her family decline. Well, like Mother, Cookie had hidden a piece of my life from me. No matter, that's behind us. Now I'll be entering the life that Mother had hidden from both of us. In no way did I sense I had her permission to do this, but death had freed her from her past and now the Huchulaks could be my family too.

I find myself backtracking through the years, thinking about what I already knew. From Bradford, Pennsylvania, we moved to Greensboro, North Carolina, and then to New Jersey where Ed, our youngest child was born. We stayed for twenty-four years. During their college years, our older children drifted in and out of the house. I drifted too -- in and out of temporary jobs, unable to focus. In New Jersey, far from Mother, buried thoughts of my real father, Hans Pederson, began to intrude.

I remember that time in New York when Aunt Helen stayed with Cookie and me while Mother met Dad in California after he returned from his final China trip. I feel again the shock I felt when Aunt Helen mentioned my father's extensive art collection, large enough to require a double penthouse for display. Then there was my Oklahoma visit to Aunt Alice when she'd said, "Your father was a very wealthy man. You were his only child. Why everyone in the family knows you're an heiress." Both of Mother's sisters, Alice and Helen, remembered my father's kindness when he'd brought them to Seattle before I was born. I recall now, the days in New York when Dad would crow, "Doris. Here's a letter from Padden and Moriarty." When I'd asked Mother who they were, she'd said, "My lawyers in Seattle."

How could I learn more? Mother's sisters had told me everything they knew, or at least whatever they'd felt they could reveal. What about Padden and Moriarty, the Seattle law firm Mother had used to settle my father's estate? I resolve to investigate. One afternoon in New Jersey, I climb the stairs to the third floor of the library and walk to the back corner under the eaves. There I find the shelves that hold the major U.S. city phone directories. In the Seattle yellow pages, under attorneys, I find one Padden and two Moriartys.

Once again I do nothing. I don't know what to do. It's 1983. Is it too late to call these lawyers and ask if they had handled Hans Pederson's affairs in 1933? Should I tell them that I, his daughter, want to learn more about my father 50 years later? If they haven't disposed of those records, finding them might entail a lengthy, costly search. Chip and I are paying college tuitions and planning our daughter Beth's wedding. I can hear the cash register "ca-ching," but these secrets continue to haunt me.

I fear I might break down if I call the lawyers myself, so I decide to ask our attorney to make the call. Mercer, a college classmate of Chip's, and a partner in a Philadelphia firm with a list of names that stretch around the block, agrees to see me.

My stomach flip-flops as the elevator rises swiftly to the top floor of a downtown skyscraper. I cross the thick carpet to the law office that spreads across the building's entire floor and announce myself to the stiffly-coiffed receptionist. I'd last seen Mercer in a pair of baggy shorts at a family softball game at an alumni picnic. He'd hit the ball hard enough that I was glad I'd been in the outfield. Still, one of the boys had caught the ball, thrown it to first, and put Mercer out.

Here in Philadelphia, Mercer wears a suit tailored from flannel as thick as the fabric in my old college beau Preston's trousers. He motions me to a chair by his office window. Downtown Philadelphia spreads before us, dominated by One Liberty Place, the stiletto-spiked, ebony-towered building we call Darth Vader.

I set my purse on the rug. "Mercer, I'm here because I'm trying to learn about the father I never knew. He died in Seattle when I was a baby. My mother told me he was a struggling young architect who got run down by a car and left us penniless during the Depression." Aware of my clenched fists, I loosen my fingers. "I know that's not true. There've been several hints from relatives."

Mercer makes no comment. He knows how to listen. A lifetime Philadelphia resident, he is deeply involved in civic and business affairs. Here I am asking him to look into my little issue. I wonder how much of his valuable time this could take. I had a lot of nerve coming in here. I shift my gaze to his Danish-modern credenza and admire the patina of the teakwood. We listen as the drone of a plane approaches the Philadelphia airport.

"Go on."

"I don't know how to go about this." I hand him an envelope with the addresses of the one Padden and two Moriartys. "These were my mother's Seattle lawyers back in 1933."

"Hey, no problem. I'll look into it." He opens the envelope and sets it on his lap.

"It's just that there's always been this undercurrent of lies and secrecy in my family. It's really bugging me."

"Of course it is." He stands and reaches for a directory on the top shelf of his bookcase. "I expect I'll find the firm in here." He pats the directory. "I expect I'll just have to make a phone call."

He graciously walks me to the elevator, giving me the feeling that I am the day's top client. I feel instant relief. Finally I have acted.

Mercer calls me back to his office a week later. Again we sit and regard Darth Vader. He makes a teepee with his fingers. "Mr. Moriarty spoke to his mother. She's the widow of your mother's attorney." He moves the teepee under his chin. Regarding me over his glasses, he swallows. "Mrs. Moriarty remembers the case well. Hans Pederson was a prominent Seattle contractor, a civic leader, and a Mason. He was a trustee and a benefactor of the Seattle Danish Home, the YMCA, and the Seattle Baseball Club. He was also a patron of the arts."

Mercer pauses. He clears his throat. His voice softens, "he was admired for his vision; for his engineering and construction skills and for his efforts to keep his men employed during the Depression."

"Huh." I pick up my purse from the rug, set it on my lap, and clutch the strap with both hands. I sift through the lifetime of lies my mother has told me along with the comments of friends and relatives who assume I have been brought up with some inkling that I was the daughter of a kind and distinguished man. I suddenly feel that I know this. It immediately feels clear.

Mercer waits for me to speak.

"But what about those letters from Padden and Moriarty that used to come to Mother in New York?" I ask, trying to control the quaver in my voice.

"They contained the checks for his paintings as they were sold." Mercer sits quietly as I grasp the news. I try to swallow and fight back tears. "You can't sue your mother," he finally says. "The statute of limitations has passed."

"I would never sue my mother. My parents took care of me. They sent me to good schools. They straightened my teeth. I just wonder why she's done this." I open my purse, pull a tissue out of the cellophane packet and blow my nose. "She must figure that the best defense is a good offense. Somehow she's always made me feel that I'm the cause of all her problems."

Mercer crumples a sheet of paper, tosses it into the air, and catches it on the way down before he says, "You may well be the best thing that ever happened to her."

All these years later I realize I felt some restraint on his part that makes me wonder if he held something back. But I never had a chance to ask him. He died young.

I look back in amazement at my acceptance of Mother's tall tales, my lack of follow-up on her clues. At fifty years old, I had rolled with life's punches, raising five children through some challenging times. I'd had thirteen hospitalizations from which I'd recovered. Still I felt barely able to absorb this news.

Figuring there had been enough secrecy in the family, I told Cookie that I was neither the product of an illicit relationship, nor the child of a suicidal failure. Mother, who incessantly worried about what people would think, should have been proud of this man. Instead, she had either disparaged him or deflected my questions at every mention of his name.

"I always figured you were probably illegitimate," Cookie said. So the mystery had affected her too. But we'd never talked about it.

Why all the secrecy? Mom and Dad tried to raise their two daughters equally. Cookie was my sister. We'd shared our upbringing. Dad had drawn on his Yankee heritage to choose our schools and our lifestyle; Mother handled the tuitions and the summers in Maine. Had she thought I would try to claim this money? As time went on, she may have felt it would be wasted on me since I had not become the society matron she felt she deserved. Besides, she and Dad needed those funds for their retirement. Whatever the reason, she'd kept her secret.

As for me, I'd brushed aside Mother's fabrications as long as I could. But what a load of guilt and feeling of worthlessness I had always carried, because I never met her expectations. That feeling of betrayal made me sick inside. I tried to ignore it, but it had changed me.

I went to the hospital once again in 1984, this time it was for a hysterectomy. Our daughter Wendy got married a few months later. I had an awful time planning the wedding—forgetting things, losing things. The lies had made me sick. The lies had poisoned our family.

Meanwhile, Mother had her hands full caring for Dad. His depression worsened, because even though he lost his mobility, he didn't lose his mind. He spent the last year and a half of his life bedridden in a nursing home. Unable to escape the demented residents who wandered in and out of his room, he retreated into watching TV, still caring who the next president or senator might be. He took his anger out on Mother, berating her in loud tones during her visits. Now that he was no longer under her care, she tolerated the abuse. He lost interest in me. When I brought our daughters' wedding albums on a visit, he pushed them away and looked out the window. I left Greensboro feeling shunted aside. After feeling close to him and trying to include him, that rejection hurt more than mother's.

Poor Dad. He soon ran out of funds to pay the nursing home. Mother's worries about his assets were well founded. His pension died with him. Inflation had eroded the value of the $2,000 and $3,000 life insurance policies he had bought in the 1920s and 1930s. But the blue chip stocks he had managed for Mother provided her with a comfortable income for the rest of her days.

Mother, Cookie, and I added on to the cottage in Maine after Dad died. Mom and I had wanted to update the dark and cramped space for years, but Dad had always insisted, "It's been fine for thirty years; it'll be fine for another thirty." A Maine architect reconfigured the space so that we could add a duplex area to the original structure. Mom would have her side; Cookie and I would have our own space that we could also rent to cover the costs of upkeep.

I spent several months in Maine with Ben and Ed during the construction. Ben, a high school junior, helped the contractor. Having never tried carpentry, he soon worked like a pro as his grandfather Hans' genes emerged. Both Ben and Ed eventually made contracting and real estate their life's work.

But the costs grew as the remodeling progressed. I found an apartment when the boys went back to school and looked for a job to cover my share of the project. No one seemed to care about my editorial experience or my growing computer skills. At interviews, supervisors' faces would fall when I walked in the door. I could feel them thinking "I don't want to hire my mother." Figuring that erasing a few years would enhance my job prospects, I had a chemical face peel. Turned out I was allergic to the antibiotic ointment. When my mouth turned into a facsimile of the Nike swoosh, I hid in my rented apartment, compulsively knitting an afghan and wondering why, after all the advantages I had been offered in life, I had decided to efface myself.

So here I am in Canada, July 2009, looking forward to moving even further back in time. Five members of my own family have come to Alberta to learn about my mother's family.

The reunion begins in the Ukrainian Cultural Heritage Village near Edmonton, where more than forty cousins and their families gather for an informal lunch of cabbage soup, braided bread, and fruit compote. Cousin Mary Ann, who lives in London, stands behind me in the buffet line. I've been told she's the family historian. Her clipped black hair sets off her dark brown eyes -- eyes that appear to hold generations of wisdom.

I pick up a pastry. "My birth father died when I was an infant."

"I know that." With a wide smile she nods at the pastry platter. "That's pampushky. A filled donut. You might as well just smear it on your hips." She leads me to a table. "On one of your mother's visits back to see us, I asked her how she got through the Depression. What she told me was, 'I did what I had to.'"

Chagrinned, I look at the cement floor. Mary Ann seems to be reinforcing Mother's attitude that my father was someone to be used and discarded.

"Don't be too hard on her." She takes a spoonful of soup. "It was a desperate time."

That's exactly why I've come, I want to say. I'm here to understand. My mother never talked about it. For most of my life I've alternated between trying to learn the truth and hiding from it. Mom had always made it clear that she wanted no questions about either

Seattle or Canada. True, once my children were grown, she'd opened up in her old age with stories about her healthy lifestyle growing up on a farm. She must have wanted to pass on some family lore before she died.

Mary Ann moves on to speak with one of her nephews, and my thoughts return to the face peel.

When I get back to New Jersey again, I still can't find a job. A friend recommends a counselor. Each week I slip off my shoes and curl up in her grassy-green wing chair, a dish of strawberry paper-wrapped candies and a box of tissues on the table beside me.

"You don't seem to be thinking of what you'd really like to do," she said one day. "What did you want to be when you were a child?"

"A garbage collector." I unwrap a strawberry candy. "I guess it was the only form of rebellion I dared take. Also, I'm kind of a sloppy dresser."

The counselor smiles, her rosy complexion set off by her pink sweater. She always wears colorful clothes. Probably to cheer up her patients.

"What's really bothering me is our cottage." I wedge the candy against one cheek. "Mother and I pushed to remodel it. I keep it up. I find the renters. I pay the bills and the taxes. But I can't seem to do anything right. If I rent it, Cookie decides that's when her family wants to come. If I don't rent it, I should have, because we need the money. If I paint it, it's the wrong color. It's getting so Cookie and Mother seem to be ganging up on me."

It emerges that by taking charge of the cottage addition, I had changed the family dynamics. I had shed the Cinderella role and begun to act like a manager instead of a servant. "I feel like somebody now," I say.

The counselor smiles and nods at my breakthrough.

"One thing though. I still want to know more about my real father. I've learned that he was not only a successful man, he was also a kind and generous man."

"Why don't you bring it up with your mother? She's obviously a strong woman. I'll bet she'd like to get it off her chest."

"But she's nearly eighty. She's getting some heart and lung problems."

It hadn't slowed her down much; she kept busy with her church, art, and bridge friends. She enjoyed her life, but her lies were still hurting me. They were hurting my family. Why had she allowed me to grow up thinking that my father was a criminal, maybe even a suicide, or else a man who had abandoned her? For years I never questioned her story that he had left us penniless in the Depression. "Don't go there!" she practically shouted with her evasive responses to my questions, She revealed no secrets. The wall that grew between us finally allowed only superficial conversation.

I decide to try once again. I go to Greensboro to show Mother and Cookie the photos of the cottage renovation.

"Why don't you stay with me?" Cookie asks. "There's more room at my house."

No. My business is with Mother. One morning after breakfast, I bring her a second cup of coffee and take the plunge, "Mother, I understand that my father was a prominent and respected man in Seattle and that he left us some money."

"You were just a baby." She jumps out of her chair. "He should have had more. People owed him money. He didn't make them pay." She heads for the kitchen. "You simply have no idea." She slaps her coffee cup on the counter and shouts, "People were jumping off of buildings. They were selling apples on street corners."

"But you used to tell me he was a struggling young architect who got run down by a car and left you penniless with me to raise."

"That's a lie. I never said that. You're making that up." She shakes her head and makes a growling sound, but she recovers and goes into her Mrs. Astorbilt routine, flinging the back of her hand to her forehead like a dying diva and moaning, "I've lived too long."

On cue, I respond, "Of course you haven't. We're glad you're still so very much alive." I grab my coat, slam the door, and go out for a walk.

In that confrontation, I'd backed her into a corner. Some violence and trauma in her life had always made her feel easily threatened. Never deliberately cruel, often loving and kind, she would sometimes burst into tears over nothing and say, "I just want everything to be nice." After so many years, she may not even realize what she'd told me. That was the only time I told her what she'd done to me.

She never asked where I'd learned about my father. The following winter, she told Ben that he looked like his grandfather. She told him Hans Pederson had left her $400,000.

At the time, Ben had moved to Florida to train as a stockbroker. Mother gave him a four-inch stack of Pederson stock certificates -- the Alaska Reindeer Company, Alaska Dano Mines Company, Seattle Sadlery Company, United Orchards Company, and Harmon E. Dunham Motor Company. "Look these up and see what they're worth," she'd told him.

"Guess she's decided to release another secret," I'd said when, wondering about it, Ben had called me.

"I spent a lot of time on this," he said. "Maybe they were worth $400,000 pre-Depression, but they're worthless today."

My mind segues back to being present in Canada at my mother's family's reunion. Enough about the lies. I haven't come to Canada to dwell on old resentments and hurts. I've felt upbeat for the past eight months at the thought of meeting Mother's family, but right now all I want to do is take a nap. Jet lag. We should have added an extra day at our expensive Edmonton hotel to recuperate from the flight before we set out on this reunion. Now everyone's ready to go so we follow the crowd to the parking lot. At least in the van I can lean back against the headrest and snooze while Matt drives us to wherever. All too soon, the van slows, and Matt pulls into the Ukrainian Cultural Heritage Village area.

I didn't pay much attention to the brochure in my reunion packet, but as we walk toward the village, it suddenly comes to me that I am about to enter my mother's childhood. This village, an open-air museum, consists of buildings gathered from the surrounding communities populated by Alberta's pioneers.

We divide into three groups. Our guides, costumed as early settlers, lead us on separate tours. As we retrace our origins, the bravery of my great grandparents, Stephan and Sanxira Tokaruk begins to sink in. The Tokaruks had come to Canada from the Ukrainian municipality of Rohizna, lured by the opportunity of free land on the western Canadian plains. The Canadian government encouraged skilled farmers to develop and populate the western provinces. Immigrants from Ukraine, Germany, Hungary, Poland, Russia and Sweden swelled Canada's population by three million at the turn of the 20th century.

Knowing they would need help to clear the forest and build a home, the Tokaruks brought their three children. Before they left, they had arranged a marriage for their eldest daughter, Anna, to Wasyl Huchulak.

They reached North America in 1898, twelve years after my father, Hans Pederson, arrived in Seattle. Their first obstacle had been language. Not only could they not speak English; they could neither read nor write either English or Ukrainian. The immigration officers took one look at their papers in Cyrillic letters and assigned the anglicized name of Huchulak to my grandparents, Wasyl and Anna.

As the family crossed central Alberta on the newly completed Canadian Pacific Railway, they marveled as they passed thousands of miles of forest and thought of how wealthy they would be in this land of trees. Their story comes to life as our guide, a history student in pioneer dress and babushka, leads us through the village, organized into three time zones based on the settlement patterns of east central Alberta. The Huculaks had arrived at the end of the nineteenth century with the earliest settlers -- former serfs who chose forested land that had to be cleared before they could begin to farm their 160-acre homesteads.

Occasionally our group intersects with another, and the guides stop to speak to each other in Ukrainian. Only the children fidget during these pauses; their parents seem at home with the language.

Through the years Mother had also lapsed occasionally into Ukrainian, but she'd always said she was just tossing out a few words of her limited Russian vocabulary. She did not let on that she had been raised speaking the language.

Even her Russian words had been circumspect. She and Dad had enjoyed the pre-World War II colonial expat life with its servants and clubs. During those years, Shanghai was filled with immigrants from all over the world -- many of them White Russians. These refugees from the rule of Czar Nicholas II had fled during the Communist revolution of 1917. Former aristocrats and members of the nobility, they eked out a living in Shanghai as best they could — the men as taxi drivers, the women as "taxi dancers." Former Cossacks of the Czar taught my husband Chip to ride horses during his Shanghai childhood.

Prejudice takes many forms and evolves through the years. Often, an American businessman who married a Russian woman was stigmatized. Widows could also be suspect. Marrying a widow did nothing to help a man's career in the 1920s and 1930s.

At this reunion I am learning that my mother grew up speaking Ukrainian — similar, but considered inferior to Russian in the social class hierarchy of a refugee. She was also a widow. She must have felt threatened by Dad's intolerance. I am beginning to realize why *never look back* was her first rule and her second — *don't ask and I won't tell.*

As we continue through the Ukrainian Cultural Heritage Center, I am relieved when our guide allows a stop for questions. The Northern Canadian day is hot and dry. As we trudge along the dusty path, I berate myself for not packing a hat with a brim. No wonder this is such great farming country — this merciless sun will beat down on us until eleven o'clock tonight.

At one stop, a cousin tells me, "My father used to tease the little ones like your mother. In summer they lowered the butter down the well on a rope to keep it cool. Dad remembered your mother screaming when he threatened to tie her up with the butter."

Shock and guilt grow on me throughout the afternoon as I begin to learn about my mother's childhood. Her father Wasyl was not only a fiddle-playing storyteller, he was also the town drunk. Mother must have grown up with a desperate craving for love, kindness, and protection. Hard-pressed to demonstrate these nurturing qualities to Cookie and me, she may have rarely experienced them herself. She chose to protect us by hiding her past. Trying to deny her roots, our mother seemed an imposter. Unsure of who she had become, she struggled to mold me into something she wasn't. I never knew who I was until I set out on my own, so I'm beginning to appreciate how hard it must have been for her to acclimate. Since Anna Hushlak had despised her husband, Mother had no example to follow of a loving and successful marriage.

Our group moves on to a small onion-domed Orthodox church filled with icons. "Oh yes, Anna," another cousin says as we enter. Grandmother Anna, "Baba," had embraced religion to the point of fanaticism. Somehow that was no surprise. But I didn't know that she had borne nine children, seven of whom survived to adulthood. One baby died when Anna rolled over in her sleep and smothered the infant. No wonder Mother made herself sick with worry as I had baby after baby. Yet, from Wasyl and Anna came the families of the nearly fifty descendants I am meeting at this reunion -- teachers, entrepreneurs, artists, environmentalists, lawyers, athletes, free spirits -- a vibrant and creative group.

Our guide leads us to a burdei or buda — a sod hut. Dug into the ground and covered in thatch, it sheltered the early settlers as they cleared their heavily forested land. We crowded into the hut and breathed the damp earth smell. Entire families huddled on benches that edged the dark and claustrophobic burdeis, sometimes for days, while winter raged and temperatures plunged to -40° on the Alberta plains. A desolate silence of boundless cold and dead whiteness brought time to a stop as wind blew the churning snow into drifts heavy enough to warm the burdei.

Anna and Wasyl had filed for title to their land in 1898, the same year that Hans Pederson probably returned to Seattle from his search for Yukon gold. To obtain title, they first had to build a house and a barn and also cultivate ten acres of their homestead land. They managed the house and barn relatively quickly, but it took five years of backbreaking labor with merely a pickaxe before they cleared the ten acres of heavily forested land and obtained their title. The Huchulaks and Tokaruks crowded into a burdei their first winter, but then abandoned it in spring when it became a dripping, covered pond. Their only choice was to move out under the stars where they contended with mosquitoes, mud, bears, and howling wolves at night.

In general, women had cleared the land and planted seeds. To earn enough to survive, many men left home for months at a time to work on the railroads, as Hans Pederson did in his early years.

Wasyl and Anna built a mud-plastered house with two large rooms. The kitchen contained a "peetch," a clay oven domed inside but flat on top. My mother, one of the younger children, had slept on the peetch during the cold winter nights. I wondered if her almost catatonic reaction to any mention of sex had come from memories of listening to her drunken father lurch home from the bar at night to make another baby while she tried to sleep beside her little siblings on the hard peetch.

Mother and Dad never agreed on property. With the exception of the cottage, Dad maintained his lifelong wanderlust, ever ready to move on and try somewhere else. Now I finally understand why Mother so badly wanted her own home.

Our reunion guide next leads us to a restored farm brought from Smoky Lake, another Ukrainian town peopled by some of my relatives. The design of the restored homestead is similar to the still-standing Huchulak homestead in Andrew that Wasyl and Anna built in 1916 when Mother was ten years old. Its south-facing entrance has windows that reach for the sun. A central hallway separates its two rooms. Warmth from the stove, which heated the home through the harsh winter, became unbearable in the summer, "which, while short, is intense with daylight that lasts until eleven at night," our guide needlessly announces. The stove had filled the house with smoke. The sister who my mother called Rose (known as Frozia to other siblings), was badly burned as a child by hot liquid from the stove.

"She was never right after that," a cousin says.

Frozia most likely watched Mother when she was little. Mother, older than her sisters Helen and Alice and her brother Alex, was ever concerned for their welfare. She must have cared for them at a very early age. It's no wonder that when I was four, she expected me to watch baby Cookie on the top bunk of the rolling ship on the day that Cookie fell to the floor and fractured her collarbone.

Many pioneer families had a summer kitchen with an outdoor stove to bake the bread as well as a root cellar for vegetables. The harsh climate and healthy diet seem to have produced Huchulak men and women of strong character and long life. Many of them lived to their late eighties and nineties with little or no medical and dental care.

We were never sure of Mother's age or the date of her birthday. She used to tell us the town records had burned. We resented her attempts to hide her age from us, ascribing "Mrs. Astorbilt's" lies and half-truths to excessive vanity. But now I am learning about the prejudice she faced. For many years, central Alberta towns neither recorded statistics on Ukrainian families, nor offered schooling to their children, believing that the town was obligated to provide an education only for English-speaking children. Since the Huchulaks and their neighbors spoke only Ukrainian, Mom's older siblings never went to school. Remaining where they were born, some of them got through life speaking only broken English.

My mother was the first in her family to go to school. I always knew she was smart, but not that she entered first grade knowing little English. No wonder she thought I would have no problem attending first grade at Sacré Coeur in the French Concession in Shanghai where the nuns conducted the school in French. Mother's younger sister Helen and her brother Alex became teachers. Alex rose to the post of vice principal of the Andrew school. Still, even with a good education, Ukrainians could find work only in Ukrainian towns. This must have been why Anna urged Mom to leave central Alberta to find a better life somewhere else. Not unusual advice. My attorney cousin, daughter of a Saskatoon farmer, told me her parents had often said, "Give the boy the farm. Give the girl an education and a suitcase."

Mom obtained a nursing degree in Edmonton, although she kept this from us as well. She hid even her accomplishments. Bright and curious, she always lip read, silently mouthing words as her finger pointed to them on the page. I never imagined that it was because she learned to read in her second language, English.

Sometimes I felt like a clotheshorse when she bought us new clothes. She'd check our feet under the x-ray machine whenever we bought shoes at New York's Best & Co. and lecture us on the importance of proper fit. Ashamed of her feet, misshapen and swollen with bunions and corns, she had probably grown up wearing her share of hand-me-down shoes.

How determined she was to overcome the position of her family. For years she'd wail, "How I sacrifice for you." I never understood that many of her sacrifices had occurred years before my birth. Her experience taught her to steer Cookie and me toward successful people as our chance for a better life. With a smile, she'd say, "I've been rich and I've been poor. Rich is better." As for me, bent on protecting myself from her arrows, I never noticed her pain.

———

Although Mother was one of the middle Huchulak children, I am the senior cousin at the reunion. I stop in the gift shop as we leave the Cultural Heritage Center and buy two pysanka, intricately patterned Ukrainian eggs. At the Royal Glenora Club banquet that night, I speak at length to cousin Mary Ann Hushlak who lives in London. Mary Ann, probably twenty years my junior, is considered the family historian because of her interest in the entire clan. Whenever I have a question, a cousin says, "Ask Mary Ann." She explains great swaths of family history to me. She'd always felt an affinity with my mother, she said, because in spite of being more than a generation apart, both of them took the risk of leaving Canada for something better. Mary Ann makes frequent visits home as Mom did in her later years. She believes, rightly, that hard as they tried, neither she nor Mother was able to leave their native country completely behind.

Mary Ann explains the burden that Mother and Aunt Alice put on her father, their brother Alex Hushlak. Both sisters denied that Anna, "Baba," was their mother. Both sisters made Alex call her "Great Aunt Anna." Anna, true to her Ukrainian peasant roots, spent her days in a shapeless black dress, her hair covered by a babushka, her thick legs encased in black stockings that covered the clotted varicose veins she developed from bearing nine children. Baba was as much an object of shame to Mother and Alice as their drunken father, Wasyl had been.

Mother brought Cookie along on one visit to Canada. One afternoon, Mom announced to Alex that she wanted to go to the cemetery. Alex shot Mary Ann a look, letting her know that it was time for the lie. So Mary Ann walked Cookie to the graves at one end of the cemetery while Alex took Mother to Anna's grave at the other end.

Alex hated the lies. Still, there was no denying that Anna was difficult. In her old age, she remained near Alex's family in the 1916 homestead. In time she became so irascible that she ruined the family's Christmas celebrations.

The morning after the banquet, we Huchulaks gather at the 1916 homestead. Only the outer shell of the house remains; the rotting interior has been condemned. We gather for photos under the bright June sun that will bear down on us long into the night. The tilled earth cleared by our grand- and great-grandparents surrounds us as waves of heat shimmer in the distance over this land that in a few short months will be subjected to sheets of ice and howling blizzards.

Cousins of my generation and their children reminisce about their childhood and our grandparents. A striking difference arises when they describe grandfather Wasyl. The boys say, "He was fun. He told great stories. He was a jolly old drunk. He wasn't so bad."

The girls shudder. "Oh yes, he was."

Why? Was he physically abusive? Verbally abusive? Did he treat the grandchildren who lived in their own homes in a different manner than he had treated his own children? If he was a molester, he could have approached his own daughters when Anna wasn't there.

From my mother's recoil at physical contact and her single-minded need to escape her past, I suspect that she endured some childhood sexual trauma. Another cousin feels the same way about her mother, who suffered from mental illness. A male cousin says, "Oh, who knows? It was all so long ago." Still, it is not something a little girl would forget, however hard she tried to repress the memory.

The girls could not have received much protection from Anna. While she hid her children in the haystack to shelter them from Wasyl, she wasn't always around when they visited him in the granary. Still, Mother spoke fondly of her father's singing, storytelling, and fiddling. She mentioned her own mother only once, the time when I brought out a family tree book in Greensboro. The time when she said that her mother told her to leave Alberta and make something of herself.

When Anna could no longer tolerate Wasyl's abuse, she divorced him; unheard of in the 1920s. She was awarded most of the property. Wasyl converted a nearby granary into a home for himself. Still, Anna could not escape Wasyl since he passed her house every night, singing as he lurched home from the tavern.

243

Even Wasyl's death was a disgrace. There came a time when the local tavern blacklisted him. After that, he had to walk two and a half miles to a bar in another town and bum rides home when it closed. One Saturday night he feigned illness, lay down in the road and rolled in the dust hoping someone would give him a ride home. Instead, a trucker who failed to see Wasyl ran over him.

Anna surprised her children when she shed copious tears at Wasyl's funeral. "So then. Are you finally sad that he is gone?" one of them asked.

"No," she replied in Ukrainian. "I am sad that he didn't die twenty-five years ago."

————

Rose Huculak is the honored guest throughout the reunion. Daughter-in-law of Wasyl and Anna, twenty years younger than her husband Nikolai, their eldest son, Rose is the only living spouse of Wasyl's and Anna's children. The next day, as we squint into the sun under the cloudless sky at the derelict homestead, eighty-eight year old Rose, seated on her walker before us, describes her early-married life with Nikolai in the two-room Huchulak homestead. After their marriage, Anna moved into the living room with its colorful wall rugs. Their intricate red patterns added a layer of warmth and a dash of color -- a contrast to the bleak gray and white landscape with its raging winds. Anna and her mother Sanxira had woven those rugs years before on a loom in the granary after the spring grain went to market.

Anna gave the newlyweds her bedroom, but she kept walking in and out without knocking on the door. It wasn't until Nick and Rose's son, my cousin Delmor was born, that Anna moved to a nearby building. Then Rose was on her own as she built a new life with Nikolai and tiny Delmor. In winter, she had to scrape six inches of ice off the windows and melt it indoors over the fire to make Delmor's bath water.

As Anna packed up her chickens for market one day, Rose asked, "Could I have a couple of chickens to start my own flock?"

Anna refused. Later, after Rose acquired her own flock, Anna got rid of her own chickens and stole Rose's eggs. She sold them and either gave the money directly to the church, or added to the church's collection of icons. Known only by their clothing to the mostly illiterate population, these picturesque icons filled the church and faced east.

After listening to Rose's history, we move to the Andrew Ukrainian Orthodox Church where the entire Huchulak family is buried in the churchyard cemetery. We learn that it took many years for Anna to save for her life's crowning achievement -- a concrete crypt to contain her mortal remains. The crypt rests conspicuously above the ground among the cracking gravestones in the little Andrew churchyard, with its old headstones of concrete and newer ones of polished granite. Anna's polished granite headstone above her concrete crypt commemorates her eighty-eight years on this earth from 1879 to 1967. Etched on one side in English and the other in Ukrainian, both sides of the headstone bear the characteristic Ukrainian slanted crosspiece below the stem of the main cross: reminders of the sacred to passersby who invariably stopped to cross themselves or pray at the crosses that served also as property markers or roadside shrines.

Families gather at these small cemeteries for picnics on Orthodox Easter, a custom reminiscent of Mexico's Day of the Dead. How I wish that I could join my newfound family on Easter to participate in this custom!

Wasyl is buried at the other end of the cemetery from Anna. She left all her money to the church. Although she purchased her crypt forty years before she died, she bought the wrong size. Her crypt was too small.

"When the time came, we had to load her in sideways," explained one of her grandchildren.

Yet Anna's piety had a strange and dramatic ending. Shortly after she was interred in her aboveground crypt, lightning struck the church to which she had devoted her life. The building, which burned to the ground, has since been rebuilt.

Modern-day headstones of Huchulaks, Huculaks, and Hushlaks point to the family's prosperity. Mother's sister Helen outlived three husbands. Her stone merely bears the name, Huculak That is all the family inscribed. Nikolai's monument, etched with his years on this earth from 1901-1989, bears the words *"Forever Remembered."* Resting beside it in 2009, Rose's headstone is inscribed with *"Forever Loved"* at its base, along with her birthdate of 1920. She knows where she will go when her time comes. This is a family that knows where it belongs.

The growing clan eventually diverged on the spelling of their given names as well as their surnames. Mary Ann explains that

Ukrainian-Canadian children were often named for an Orthodox saint whose birthday was near their own. My mother came next in birth order to the sister she called *Rose*, known as *Frozia*, the diminutive of the saint, *Eufrosina*. The name on Mother's birth certificate is *Domka Huchulak*. The graduation certificate from her Edmonton nursing school lists her as *Anna Dorris Huchlak*. (a fourth Hushlak spelling.) In his will, my father spelled her name as *Dorris*. She then called herself *Doris Ann Pederson*. According to Mary Ann, Mother's birth name of *Domka* could have been the diminutive of the saint *Eudochia, Edvokia, or Eudokia*, a name used in Russia as well; or of *Teodora*, the mother of a Byzantium emperor.

I expect Mother told us the town records burned, because she was ashamed to reveal that for some years she actually knew neither her given name nor her age. She did say that she decided to leave Alberta and make her own way instead of marrying one of the local farmers. Mom was pleased when I told her, late in her life, that she should be proud of her family and their achievements. Still, she rarely spoke of her childhood.

People leave their homeland for different reasons. Tragic are the refugees who flee for their lives with only the clothes on their backs. A refugee from the Hungarian uprising of 1956, expelled by Russian tanks whose guns mowed down people in the Budapest streets, once asked me, "Why do Americans object to being taxed for defense? Can you understand what it is like to cower in hiding while you watch your children, your parents, your neighbors, gunned down in the street before your eyes? Why, your defense tax costs you no more than one of your car payments."

Immigrants such as my parents are more likely to feel trapped in a land with no opportunity. They take huge risks to search for a better life where they hope to prosper and create a new home. They must look ahead.

————

My cousins, Judy Shulko and Genevieve Huculak, compiled a family history after the reunion. Genevieve honored the legacy of our grandparents when she wrote:

"In spite of his problems with alcohol, Wasyl has given his descendants his artistic talents, his sense of humor, his generosity of spirit, and love of family.

"Anna has given her descendants an entrepreneurial savvy, a strength of spirit to overcome obstacles, and a fearless sense of adventure to explore new places and take on new enterprises."

Like Wasyl, Mother loved her family. But the experiences of her early years left her with an instinct for survival, secrecy and a need for control. The position of her birth family crippled her. Like her mother Anna, she endured. She raised Cookie and me with advantages beyond her dreams. As she told my cousin Mary Ann, "I did what I had to." She did it over and over and never looked back.

Mother inherited Anna's bluntness and cunning, her lack of patience, and her greed — or possibly a compulsion to squirrel away funds for potential disaster. Like many pioneer women, Anna turned in desperation to religion, hoping the icons she gave to the church would guarantee her salvation in an afterlife. Instead of collecting icons, Mother collected Chinese objects and counted her gold. At the end of her life she was obsessed with distributing the belongings that she considered her legacy. Once I had them, I sold most of them. My dealer understood, relieving pangs of guilt. "Old objects accumulate baggage," he said. "Change is healthy."

Anna convinced Mother that she had a higher destiny than marriage to one of the local farmers. Adventurous Domka followed her mother's advice. Still, how frightening it must have been to turn her back on her home, her family, and her culture in the midst of desperate economic times.

While she was alive, I protected myself from her arrows. It was only after she died that I began to understand that she never found closure to the tragedies of her life. She saw herself as a sacrificial lamb who had escaped, only to lose again. Hoping to be the wife of two successful husbands, she became their caretakers. Hoping to be the mother of two successful daughters, she believed that we settled for mediocrity. Lost in her regard was any esteem for the outstanding man responsible for her wealth and my life.

19. The Arctic Club

I pick up *The New York Times* one afternoon in my dentist's waiting room shortly after the Huchulak reunion. Leafing through its pages, I notice an article that announces the opening of the Arctic Club Hotel in downtown Seattle. Designed by Architect A. Warren Gould, the 1917 building was one of the first to use terra cotta panels over a steel reinforced concrete frame. Behind the registration desk, the clerk in the photo stands next to a glass dome stacked with stiff round collars, a detail that lends a Victorian touch to the building recently designated as a National Trust Historic Hotel.

"Whooo," I blurt. The paper drops into my lap, prompting a wary look from the other waiting patients. Am I scheduled for a root canal? No, my outburst has been caused by a sudden "aha" moment. This Arctic Club has to be the one that my father built in 1917, the building closed for renovations that Don and I had tried to visit on my Seattle trip two years earlier. The building is located half a block from the six-story King County Courthouse where a bronze plaque commemorates Hans Pederson's work as the general contractor.

I fold the page for a second look. Within *The New York Times* photo are smaller framed photos on the wall behind the registration desk — photos of the club's founding members: men associated with the Klondike Gold Rush of 1897-98. Under their vests and suit coats the men wear shirts with the same starched round collars that I see stacked under the glass dome. My father, a lifelong club member and a Klondike gold rush prospector, would surely be one of these men.

I have to see it. Chip and I need to make another trip to Seattle so we can stay at the Arctic Club Hotel. I want to find my father's photo on the wall behind the registration desk. I must explore that building. This time we will search for other buildings, bridges, and roads that that my father built. We will experience the city as it was. We should also explore second-hand bookstores. Somewhere in my research, I've learned that Olaf Linck, a Danish medical illustrator, published a Danish biography about Hans Pederson in 1930: *Kong Hans ved Stillehavet ("King Hans at the Pacific Ocean.")* Finding this book will surely help me understand who my father was as well as what he did. Maybe I can get to know him as a real person — know him as more than some Zeus or Thor, who early in the 20th century had supposedly reigned over the Seattle contractors from the summit of Mt. Rainier.

On a wintry afternoon in 2010, our taxi driver pulls to a stop at The Doubletree Arctic Club Hotel at 3rd & Cherry in downtown Seattle, shoving his parking brake to keep the car from rolling back down the hill. I recognize the building from my downtown excursion with Don two years earlier. That morning I had awakened with a migraine after seeing my father's photo heading Victor White's article, *Seattle's Little Known Dynamo*. Now, I step out of the taxi and, as Chip pays the driver, I look up and take in the magnificent edifice. Outside the third floor, those terra cotta walrus heads, tusks curving low, guard the building's perimeter through heavy-lidded eyes.

"Is something wrong?" the clerk asks me as Chip signs the hotel register. Evidently my disappointment shows once I've scanned the founding members' photos mounted on the wall behind the desk. My father's now-familiar face is not among them. Both his *Seattle Times* and *Seattle Post Intelligencer* obituaries, as well as comments in newspaper articles, had stated that he built the Arctic Club.

"He might be downstairs," the clerk says. "Those walls are lined with members' photos too."

First we get settled. Our room welcomes us as if we are about to set out for the Klondike. Two enlarged sepia photos of fur-hooded Alaskans, their faces weathered by hardship, regard us with stoic patience from the wall behind the bed. Leather-cornered nightstands that resemble old suitcases stand on either side of the bed awaiting our provisions. I switch on the floor lamp and notice an Arctic map embedded in the parchment shade. Soon, a knock on the door brings the concierge to welcome me, the daughter of the contractor, with a bottle of wine and a fruit and cheese tray.

I settle into the leather armchair, put my feet on the hassock and cradle the little plush walrus they've left between the pillows on the bed. Chip finds a corkscrew, pops the cork and pours two glasses of Merlot.

253

I have returned to the club of my father. The club he built for his intrepid prospecting colleagues.

On my second glass of Merlot, I begin to plan another trip to Seattle. Next winter in Maine, I'll begin training with Frosty and a team of sled dogs. I've seen these teams after Portland blizzards circling Back Bay around the Marginal Way. "Mush," I'll shout as I crack the whip and listen to it whiz over the heads of my dogs, who will speed up in response to its whine — because, of course, I'll never actually whip my dogs. As part of my compilation of odd and useless facts, I have gathered lore on arctic dog training and feeding. Will I pick up raw beef at the supermarket after they run? Will it spoil them? They might not get much meat on the trail. Maybe the fish market carries seal blubber. Anyway, I'll bring my well-trained team to Seattle where we'll get outfitted for the challenge ahead. Since the gold is gone in Dawson City, we'll enter the Iditarod. Hah! My fantasy bursts as I admit we won't last five minutes even if we get to Alaska. Just the same, I like the Arctic Club. I celebrate my father enjoying good times here with good friends.

We set out to explore the hotel. The recent renovations have recaptured the ambience of a gentleman's club. Dark woodwork and paneling surrounding the lobby invite the weary traveler to sink into one of the brown leather club chairs or else warm himself in front of the massive fireplace. Subdued conversation and laughter coming from the well-dressed crowd around the sweeping bar attest to the hotel's popularity as a watering hole.

Red carpet covers the marble stairs to the second floor. Another disappointment. Clinton Hyde's 1978 article notes, *"Entering from Cherry*

Street today, one can see 'Hans Pederson' stamped in the concrete at the foot of the marble stairs." Tight carpet blankets the stairs today, so there is no way to unearth the Pederson stamp. Turning right at the top of the stairway, we reach the elegant second-floor dome room, so named for the massive stained glass dome that serves as a ceiling. The concierge tells us that during a 1949 party when an earthquake struck, the chandelier lighting the center of the room swayed until it almost crashed into the dome. Neighboring buildings cracked, but not the steel-framed Arctic Club. The chain on the chandelier was lengthened during renovations to protect the dome in the event of another earthquake.

Chip takes the steps two at a time and I hurry behind him to the lower level to scan the downstairs walls for my father's photo. The HistoryLink.org *Encyclopedia of Washington State History* notes that the Third Avenue side of the Arctic Club was set aside as commercial office space. Passing through a cigar store in the lobby, engineers, businessmen, and city workers rode elevators to their offices. My civic-minded father no doubt frequented the fifth floor offices of the Chamber of Commerce and the Commercial Club.

A headache flickers at my temples as we reach the elevators. We've come all this way, but there is no photo of my father. Should I believe Clinton Hyde, who was not only the executive secretary of the Seattle/King County Visitors Bureau, but also secretary of the Danish Consulate? His 1978 article stated:

"A life member of the Arctic Club, Hans Pederson was proud of the home he built for the club at Third Avenue and Cherry Street in 1917. It was here, either in the lounge on the first floor, or under the opulent domed ceiling of the dining room that he was sometimes greeted by other members as 'King Hans.'"

Hyde titled his article, Forgotten Contractor Left Imprint -- in Sidewalks. *The Seattle Times* obituary noted that Pederson's name "is engraved in sidewalks, on roads, on the sides of buildings, on cornerstones, in every section of Seattle and wherever else in the Northwest his industry extended." Clearly he wanted to be remembered for his work. Perhaps we've missed some corner of the building, but we've had no more success finding his photo at the Arctic Club than I had when we searched for his "imprint" in the sidewalk two years earlier when I explored the underground sidewalks with Wendy and Matt. Victor White, who wrote the 1973 Pederson tribute, Seattle's Little Known Dynamo, surely chose a good title for his article. No record seems to exist that my father was even a member of one of his best-known buildings just half a block from the courthouse where a bronze plaque at the entrance credits him as the contractor.

Hyde and White wrote their articles more than forty years after Pederson's death. Although White had known my father years earlier, parts of his article were based on hearsay. Here's what someone told him about my mother and me:

"She knows her business. She nurses and fusses over him unbelievably. Did you ever know anybody who didn't love Hans? We're all genuinely jealous of the Old Man …

Two or three years after their marriage, his wife went to the hospital and brought home a baby boy... A couple of years later, I stopped and asked about Pederson.

'He's getting along fine,' they told me. 'Mrs. Pederson brings the boy in once in a while. We all love the kid and he looks so much like the Old Man, we're just waiting for him to grow up and take charge.'"

White didn't bother to read Pederson's 1933 obituaries. Both state that my father left a nameless bride and an infant daughter, Paula. Still, whatever White's fabrications, I still treasure his *Frontier Times* article because of the outstanding photo of my father beside the title, *Seattle's Little Known Dynamo*.

My mother had a hard childhood. She did the best she could for us — don't we all? It appears that one reason she obliterated my father's contribution to our lives was a desire for revenge. She seemed to believe that Hans Pederson was a bad man who abandoned her by dying before he collected what was owed him. His tenants who failed to pay their rent, his employees who couldn't feed their children, his customers and his charities; all of them were competitors who deprived her of her rightful inheritance. She felt he had betrayed her. To her, neither his work nor his example, but only his assets were his sole worthwhile legacy. Never able to overcome her early memories, she could only measure her worth by her possessions. He achieved his by the way he lived. Her revenge was to keep him a secret from me.

———

I soon imagine myself a member of the Arctic Club. We walk each day to the King County Courthouse half a block away, passing a yawning hole in the ground as we go back and forth. Whatever building had once stood between the Arctic Club and the King County

257

Courthouse had been demolished, leaving only an unsightly, rubble-filled excavation. To me, it seems like a murder. That structure must have been built by one of my father's colleagues.

Once we reach the courthouse entrance and pass Hans Pederson's name on the bronze plaque, security screens us before we are allowed to tap across the Alaskan marble floors to continue our unsuccessful search for other legal documents about my father. Old court records relating to the eight-year legal battle on the estate may have been moved to another building, we are told. Padden and Moriarty sent Mother 233 pages of letters and records pertaining to the estate. Someone tore out thirty-five of them. Were those pages a record of other assets? Other liabilities? It seemed not. Those monthly statements documented financial records over and over during the eight years of conflict over the settlement. I decide my mother must have torn the pages out, although I still don't know why. I let it go. What my father did is more important to me than what he left.

We spend two more days traipsing around the downtown, soaking up the atmosphere of old Seattle. Waiting in line at downtown restaurants, loquacious Chip, who has never met a stranger, tells people our story. Everyone seems interested. Seattleites are proud of their city. We then learn we are too late. I seem to have reached another dead end in the search for my father.

Maybe I can find his biography, *Kong Hans ved Stillehavet.* There has to be a copy somewhere among Seattle's large Scandinavian population. We ride trolleys to several second-hand bookstores. No one has ever heard of the book.

On our last day, Chip zips up his suitcase in our Arctic Club room and says, "We haven't tried the public library. After all, they got you started in the first place."

"We should have brought our hiking boots," he says as we trudge up the hill to Fifth Avenue, passing a little iron railing that marks a partially sunken sidewalk. As we round the corner to the library, a fantastic structure appears before us; a set of cubes that appears to have been dropped onto the sidewalk from another galaxy. Wikipedia describes the eleven-story library building as "several discrete floating platforms seemingly wrapped in a large steel net around glass skin."

We step off the elevator and hail a reference librarian who heads for his computer, slides into a chair, and begins to tap the keys as he says, "I expect we'll find the book in World Cat."

Sure enough, it is in the world catalog. Six copies of *Kong Hans ved Stillehavet* are known to exist in Denmark and six in the U.S. -- five in university libraries and one in the New York Public Library. Other copies surely exist in Seattle. I expect that my generous father purchased several of these books if for no other reason than to reward the enterprising author who traveled in 1929 from Denmark to Seattle to interview him for his biography during a year of rampant bank and business failures.

Finally, after three months of correspondence with U.S. libraries, the University of Alaska at Fairbanks releases their copy to me through interlibrary loan.

20. I Meet My Father

Olaf Linck, author of *Kong Hans ved Stillehavet*, paid an extended 1929 visit to Hans and Marie Pederson to gather material for a biography he published in 1930 in Denmark. Casting about for a moneymaking project, Linck, a medical illustrator, may have persuaded the Danish government to underwrite his book during the roller-coaster year of 1929. In his preface, he is frank about his choice of Pederson as a subject. Linck had written an earlier biography of Laurits Andersen, another successful Dane, "Who grew rich teaching the Chinese to smoke cigarettes." Unknown in Denmark until after his death, Laurits Anderson left his entire fortune to the Danish Government. They used it to create a fund for the promotion of trade and industry. Hans Pederson, another aging Dane who left Denmark in his youth with "empty pockets," had risen to prominence in Seattle. Since he and Mrs. Pederson had no heirs, Linck may have hoped that a praiseworthy biography would entice Pederson to follow Andersen's example and leave his fortune to the Danish nation.

Having completed much of his work by then, my sixty-five-year-old father to be reminisced with Linck about both his life and his work on a series of outings. Linck toured the city and the countryside with Hans and Marie Pederson during his visit. He cast them in a flattering light, portraying them not only as central figures in Seattle's Danish colony of 2,500 but also as a couple with deep convictions and generous characters. He concluded that Pederson would serve as an example to others, but only if they were smart enough and tough enough to overcome difficulties.

Linck brings Pederson to life as he describes his personality, his mannerisms, and his philosophy. Since he wrote his story in a "you are here" style, I feel welcome to tag along. My father seems almost to speak to me as together we move ahead to the past. The man behind the myth begins to emerge.

———

Approaching Seattle, a city of 500,000, from Glacier National Park, Linck marvels at the paradise visible from the window of the train as it passes through jagged rocks split by the dynamite blasts that formed a passage for the railroad tracks. Soon the view shifts to wildflower-dotted meadows. Continuing on, they pass fruit and dairy farms, until suddenly Mt. Rainier looms through the clouds. Linck observes that the Danish farmers who move their cows at the foot of the mountain never dreamed of such glory when they lived in Denmark as peasants and servicemen.

Linck gets settled at the Butler Hotel, then heads for Pederson's office where he introduces me to my father as I read about this man whose ruddy cheeks and benevolent eyes show him to be entirely Danish. A well-proportioned man in his mid-sixties, he has thick white hair and piercing blue eyes. He sets his horn-rimmed glasses on his desk when Linck arrives and shifts the conversation from English into Danish.

He motions Linck toward a chair beside the window before he returns to the phone. Between calls, he swings back and forth in his swivel chair and speaks with two cement contractors who stand, hats in hand, at his desk. He takes no notes. The walls are covered with photos of Pederson's buildings; an impressive collection of stones, cement, and steel.

One photo rests beside the phone on Pederson's desk. It is his son — who had met an early death — a young laughing man with strong white teeth. Above the photo hangs a poster with the words, GET YOUR HAPPINESS OUT OF YOUR WORK OR YOU WILL NEVER KNOW WHAT HAPPINESS IS.

———

Linck's description of my father is the way I have pictured him at the pinnacle of his career. Yet the curious juxtaposition of his working philosophy above the photo of his spirited young son who died at nineteen, strikes me as a cry of pain. A real person begins to emerge from the adulation posted in print.

Hans was born at his grandparents' farm home in Stenstrup on Denmark's Isle of Fyn, where his grandfather worked as a day laborer on the Lojtved estate. Hans' father, Christian Pedersen, left Stenstrup shortly after Hans' birth in 1864. His mother, Gjertrud Hansen, a maid servant at various farm houses, moved to Vester Aaby a few months after Hans was born.

Hans' grandparents raised him in their tidy home where potted plants lined the windowsills and a garden grew beside the house. In her poignant compilation of oral histories, *New Land, New Lives, Scandinavian Immigrants to the Northwest,* Janet Rasmussen documents the probable lifestyle of the Pedersen family. Farming on the windswept island heaths brought survival, but little else. At home there was enough to eat: milk, butter, and cheese from the cows, beets, carrots, rutabagas, and potatoes from the root cellar, which also cooled the dairy products in the summer. Peat moss from bogs kept the roof thatched, but the daily tasks necessary for survival left no time for play. Both my father and my mother shared similar childhoods and diets on the working farms where they were raised. But unlike the Huchulaks, motivated by the future they could build as homesteaders, the Pedersens were tenant farmers who worked the lands of the manor homes that dotted the Isle of Fyn.

Janet Rasmussen describes the childhood of Martin Rasmussen, another Dane raised on a farm. Each morning, Martin steered the cows out to the field before school. He pulled rutabagas and turnips once he got home. The entire family helped during potato harvest by digging a hole and lining it with straw

264

to store the potatoes. Some of them rotted. The family thatched the roof and cut straw for the horses by hand. Women milked the cows three times a day and did the sewing, laundry, and cooking in between. Everyone sat down to a dinner of side pork and potatoes.

At age seven, Hans entered the country school with eight other boys and three girls. He attended every other day until he was fourteen, His formal schooling at an end, he was then confirmed in the Stenstrup Church. Soon after, he went to work as a servant at a farm at Krarup Parish, eight kilometers from home.

Life in Stenstrup offered either the prospect of dependence on a feudal lord or else a low-paying job in some failing industry. My father had read of a Danish American who returned to Denmark a rich man after buying and selling farmland. So, once he completed his required military service, he sank his savings into a third class ticket to America and crossed the Atlantic in 1884. After a brief stint working for a New York State farmer he turned toward the Midwest and settled in Lamberton, Minnesota during the peak of Scandinavian immigration. There he earned sixteen dollars a month as a farm laborer, twice what he had earned in Denmark.

Too ambitious to remain in any of Minnesota's established Scandinavian settlements, Pederson continued west, working on buildings. He constructed an entire house by himself, and from this learned to calculate materiel costs. He realized he would earn more profit taking the risk as contractor while letting others perform the labor.

He worked his way west on the Northern Pacific Railroad the following summer, making himself sick from overwork. He found port work in Seattle, and also a roommate. Once he had saved $100, he deposited it in a bank, and when he accumulated $200, he began to send money to his family in Denmark — a practice he continued throughout his life. By then his mother Gjertrud had married Hans Jensen, a headmaster at a workhouse for the poor in Vester Aaby. Their marriage brought Hans two half-sisters and a half-brother.

Like other Scandinavians, Hans reveled in the forest, fishing, and farming opportunities of the Pacific Northwest. Danes excelled at dairy farming. They formed coops, then established the Danish Brotherhood in 1888. Twenty years later, Pederson built Washington Hall at 14th and East First Street to serve as their headquarters.

———

Linck fills in many of the gaps I've wondered about as he reminisces with my father on a country drive. He describes the glorious landscape dominated, as ever, by Mt. Rainier: *"The lactating breast, which sends her life-making flow over the land."* They pass an occasional red building against the forest backdrop, then ride along a river with pink sand beaches and icy waters. My father has hired a driver. Since his fortunes rise and fall, he notes, he's never bothered owning a car. He seeks challenge, not possessions.

They stop at one of his two-hundred-acre farms, run by a young Danish couple who are raising barley, alfalfa, and peas. Many times he provided seed money for the purchase of a farm. Once the tenant developed it to profitability, he would reimburse Pederson. Since Pederson conducted business without written contracts, neither his generosity nor the final ownership is found in official records. The farm provides everything needed for a life on the land: forest and meadow for rooting pigs, two horses, a dozen cows, lambs and hens; even turkeys and ducks. My father leaves the car and inspects a new silo under the construction of Danish artisans.

"Do not go too far," says Mrs. Pederson. "It will not be long before dinner is ready." She turns to Linck. "He is restless. He can't help it."

He soon returns to the car and gets back on the road. "It is a hobby," he says. "Farming is not enough for a man to think about. I acquired this farm last year, and the earth is not yet properly cleared."

"Why all these farms?" Mrs. Pederson asks. "When we could come and go and shut the door for a holiday, wasn't it enough?"

"It can get you good," the builder replies good-naturedly. Ordering the driver to stop again, he dashes into the meadow with Linck in pursuit. "It is since our son died," my father explains. "The wife misses him so much that she finds it hard to live." He finds a cherry tree and picks from the low branches. "She has severe ailments in recent years. She is tormented by gout."

On the way back to Seattle they stop at Broadmoor, Pederson's showcase farm, with seventy dairy cows. "It was expensive to get started, but I now can pay Chris, my nephew, two hundred dollars a month to run it." Broadmoor is now an exclusive area of Seattle.

Linck observes that Pederson has a big heart when it comes to giving a chance to people who want to work. I'll say -- his nephew Chris must have had a large family to earn two hundred a month in 1929. On my first post-college job in 1955, I also earned two hundred dollars a month for office work.

Back in Seattle, they ride the elevator to the City County Building, (later renamed the King County Courthouse). As low bidder, Pederson has seventy weeks to complete the $2,110,000 project before a daily fine accrues, so he hustles to make up for lost time. He dashes out of the elevator as they reach the roof. Linck follows with a stranger who confides, "Pederson is the youngest man in Seattle."

He stops to speak in Danish to workers who are filling the steel frames with cement. Even after forty years in the US, it seems he never says no to a countryman looking for work. They race up the sidewalk toward the Arctic Club on the steep corner of Third and Cherry Streets. Linck notes that "Hans Pederson" stands written in brass letters in the cement front of the building.

———

So, he did build the Arctic Club! Later a friend found his photo in a corner of the hotel that we had missed. He left his mark on other downtown projects as well. His logo, stamped at the intersections of his many sidewalks, later cracked and crumbled as his assets did, pulled and hammered by his creditors and competing relatives; his legacy sinking like the Seattle streets, suppressed by the bitterness of his second wife, my mother.

———

Looking northward, Linck hears noise, noise, noise as the city expands. He shifts his gaze to the east where the cable tram pushes up the hills, giving Linck the strange feeling that the traffic will roar down on his head.

I join them at the Arctic Club for lunch as an invisible onlooker. With a friendly slap across the shoulder, the crowd greets my father sometimes as Hans, sometimes by his nickname, King Hans. Linck observes that these businessmen with suntanned faces and direct glances appear more robust than East Coast Americans. My father motions Linck toward one of the Chesterfield chairs before the fireplace, then leaves him as he continues his business.

Aware that Prohibition has been the law in Washington for thirteen years, Linck observes several patrons ordering drinks at the extended bar across the lobby. Hunter, a member seated next to him, explains the situation. Before Prohibition, Hunter drank water, but now he flouts the law by placing a monthly order with his bootlegger for any type of prohibited spirits. Hunter's bootlegger may have been Roy Olmstead, a rumrunner who supplied booze to the Arctic Club. J. Kingston Pierce notes in *Eccentric Seattle* that Olmstead would "*Send shipments right up to the city's main docks, off-loading booze into trucks marked 'meat,' 'fresh fish,' or 'occidental bread,' and laugh heartily as 'bought' cops conveniently turned their heads.*"

"The prohibition law is an insult to all freedom-loving and healthy men," Hunter says. "Why should the Government tell me what I am allowed to eat and drink in my own home?" Hunter slaps the arm of his chair. "The State has committed an assault against me. My house is my castle -- in the United States we are not serfs to the lords."

Linck concludes that Prohibition offers another enticing, risk-taking opportunity to the west's intrepid pioneers.

Finding a table in the dining room, Pederson returns to Linck and says, "When my wife is better, you must see our home at the top of Highland Drive. Today I cannot give you eggs and pork, but oh, she is a fine cook when she is healthy."

Their order is taken by "Cannonball," an elderly black and bald waiter, named not for his shining pate, but because he has been a waiter on the Cannonball train. Pederson casts an envious glance at his robust frame and says, "That man is wasted here. He should be out building bridges."

Linck decides that the Pedersons believe obstacles are put in this world to be overcome. I have felt this way myself, especially during the years when we raised our five children and I made thirteen trips to the hospital.

They move on to the bank after lunch. The director says, "Hello Hans, what can I do for you?" then hands him a check for clearing a forest to make room for new farms.

"I have four farms. One in California," my father says as they leave. "I love to see things grow in the earth."

"Do you earn something on your farms?" Linck asks.

"It depends. I lost $52,000 on one hundred acres. My cattle farms here in the neighborhood of Seattle, they go better. Keeping a

270

farm -- it is a luxury for a businessman, but I want to own places where I can spend a holiday."

They move on. A man crawls out of a long hole in the ground and bows to Pederson as they pass a viaduct under construction. Linck continues, "I've heard you are president of the Danish Old People's Home." Pederson nods. "And I've heard you delivered the work for nothing when the home was built." Linck has learned that he has to drag information out of him.

"Oh yes." My father looks around, his thoughts already elsewhere.

Linck brings him back. "I've wanted to write a book about you and your work."

Pederson smiles his good-natured, half-embarrassed smile. "I have had bankruptcy. If the work had not been assigned to me, others would have performed it." He hails a streetcar. "Come. We will go now to see a school."

Planned as a junior-high school for four hundred students, the nearly completed James Madison School needs only furniture, doorknobs and fixtures. My father points with pride to the classrooms, kitchen, cafeteria, auditorium, labs and workshops so dazzling that Linck compares them to operating rooms.

They pass a classroom where a young man is on his knees with a grinder. Pederson stops in the doorway. "He was a ship boy on a Danish steamer. One voyage was enough. He deserted and hid once they reached Seattle. I hired him at a good daily wage. I don't encourage desertion, but I have met several deserters who have gone clean. There

271

must be backbone and ambition, and a solid character to venture this dangerous experiment."

He never tires of building schools, he tells Linck. He emphasizes to young people the importance of thoroughly learning a profession. "Some lately complain that the poor are being more and more pushed out of work. They feel exploited, but in their youth they never learned a trade. It is not always their fault, but opportunity comes to those who keep their eyes open."

Late that afternoon, my father leaves Linck at the Butler Hotel with one of Bagley's volumes containing sketches of Seattle's notables. "There's something about me inside," he says over his shoulder as he leaves. Crossed out in pencil is a stranger's name printed on the business card that marks the page. Not bothering with a personal card, Pederson has written his name on the back with a note that he'll meet Linck the next day with a car.

A woman is at the wheel the next morning. "What do I need with a car?" asks Seattle's largest builder. "If the walk is far, a friend will always drive me."

Reviewing his buildings appears to be Pederson's relaxation. They pass his projects: the Ballard Locks, the Fifteenth Avenue Bridge and Smith Pier; the Fox Theater, overloaded with stucco embellishments. "They are okay," the builder says, "But I had to wait long for my money." Linck feels the forecasts and figures clicking away in my father's head as he continues, "What is important is that every Friday, workers should have their reward."

As they pass his apartment houses Linck asks, "It is remarkable, so many large inhabited buildings. Is there one too many?"

"There is no shortage. But who knows when suddenly a new situation will bring people into town? So I keep on top and do not say no to any opportunity." He directs the driver to Liberty Court, a 100-unit apartment complex for poor families with children where he has set an affordable low rent. "The contracting supervisor was a formerly prosperous Dane," he says. "He lives here now. Times are not as good as they were. I hired him because he is cheerful and makes the best of things."

Their driver ends the afternoon with a searing stop at the city jail. Prisoners of all races are mixed together in an eerie grid, their hands outstretched for a morsel or a cigarette. But it is the women's cage that stops Linck. While some Seattle histories wink at the gambling and prostitution that filled the city's coffers in collusion with the law, Linck is horrified at the silence of young women sleeping off their drunkenness and highs from "the white wife," cocaine, smuggled from China. The girls look like corpses. The Prohibition drinking orgies Linck has observed around town are nothing compared with the white poison, cocaine. When the girls wake up, they will drag themselves to bars and beg to be freed by selling their bodies.

Linck is appalled. But my father, who had lived in Seattle for forty-five years, was a builder, not a reformer. The best he could do for a man was to give him a job, a gateway to the opportunity to control his own life. He employed hard workers and risk takers like himself. To keep his men employed, his buildings ran the gamut from churches to jails, from vaudeville emporiums to exclusive clubs, from public works to private homes.

"Any job to keep his men at work, Pederson motto," ran a *Christian Science Monitor* headline in a March, 1931 article. He did not expect the city to conform to his standards.

21. Risks

My father came to Seattle in 1886, a year that offered work to everyone in the vibrant and growing west. Ambitious immigrants could prosper, send dollars back to the old country, and plan ahead for their legacies. Pederson soon had more projects than he could manage after the devastating 1889 Seattle fire. Yet looking back, he considers himself inexperienced and stupid to have worked for others and let them take the profit.

"In America nobody would do it for you," he tells Linck as they take a break on one of their excursions. He sketches the early days when he wandered over mountains and helped farmers reap their hop fields for half a dollar a day. More profitable were opportunities to clear a forest, hard work that yielded between $100 and $1,000. He went south to California where he worked in Los Angeles and San Francisco. Then he headed north to the mine district in British Columbia.

He returned to Seattle again in 1897 just as the ship, *The Portland* returned from the Yukon's Klondike River, steaming slowly into the harbor beneath a cargo of two tons of gold. In his remarkable book, *The*

Klondike Fever, the Life and Death of the Last Great Gold Rush, Pierre Berton tells the story of the final international search for gold -- a frenzy that lasted really only a year. Six weeks after *The Portland* docked, close to 20,000 people left Seattle for the Yukon. Most gold-seekers were either young Americans or immigrants, many galvanized by the chance to leave dreary jobs they had settled into after the Gilded Age recession, in addition to bankers, reporters, seamen, and doctors who also yanked their life savings out of banks in the headlong search not only for gold, but to face the challenge of the wilderness.

Nearly 100,000 prospectors, or "cheechakos" passed through the forbidding Canadian wilderness in a little over a year, with few of them prepared for the savage conditions they would meet. In an effort to control the flood, Canada passed a "one-year law" that required prospectors to pack enough supplies -- a ton in fact -- of food, blankets and mining equipment that would last them a year.

Craving freedom and adventure as well as gold, my father and a partner joined the 20,000 Seattle prospectors. Dumped on the Alaskan shore, they hastened to move their supplies to high ground before the briny waters of the incoming tide saturated them and mildew set in. Tents lined the swampy waterfront. Stepping outside brought oncoming swarms of the mosquitoes and black flies already tormenting their dogs and packhorses into madeness.

They lined up for the trip over the passes along trails worn by thousands before them—Trails clotted with jettisoned trash -- smashed sleds, rotting sacks spilling moldy flour, dead horses and dogs not yet cleaned to the bone by hungry wolves. They hurried to beat the coming snows that would soon reach depths of more than sixty feet.

The cheechakos slogged through August's matted fallen leaves toward the Chilkoot or White Pass, the two entrances to the Yukon Valley. Some may have felt comfort in their numbers as they crowded the well-worn trails that led to the Chilkoot, a treacherous gap between the spiked mountains. The almost vertical climb of 1,000 feet passed through overhanging glaciers and bottomless snow that carried the ominous thread of avalanches. Stooped under his load, each man labored to reach the Chilkoot's summit.

There they met the Canadian Mounted Police who blocked their passage until they had produced their required one year of supplies, a task that required many trips over the Chilkoot. Every man had at least one partner to spell him on the arduous climbs. Should he fall, no one behind him could afford to risk stepping off the steep trail to lend a helping hand.

Like lemmings they came, and it was mainly the vigilance of the Mounties that kept the Yukon stampede from turning into a suicide mission. Without that ton of food and supplies, many more would have perished.

Although most prospectors came from America, the paths to the gold fields led through Canada. Canadian prospectors generally came from Edmonton. While our 2009 Huchulak reunion trip included a day at the Calgary Stampede, we later learned that Edmonton sponsors the annual Klondike Days sometime during the summer.

A massive movement of people to the Northwest took place during late nineteenth century. As Hans Pederson forged his way through Canada to an Alaskan mining camp, my mother's grandparents, the Tokaruks, and her parents, the Huchulaks, claimed their homestead in Andrew. Having crossed Europe, the Atlantic Ocean and much of the North American continent, the promise of free forested land meant more to them then the considerable risk of searching for gold -- if they even knew about the gold.

Although my father told Linck that he and his partner pulled their belongings on a sled over the mountains until they reached the Yukon River mining camps, he didn't tell him that the trip probably took three months. Taking a breath seared the lungs. Tearing eyes froze eyelashes. Wet feet brought on frostbite. My father and his partner labored on slowly, as they encountered howling winds and crashing ice. They ate cold beans and fatback bacon. Dysentery, scurvy, or spinal meningitis stopped half of the prospectors. Others became disoriented by snow blindness.

The ice finally heaved its way to extinction in May. The thaw brought mud and rain. The prospectors who had readied their rafts left for the treacherous trip down the Yukon River rapids to the mining camps. Of the 100,000 who prepared to go, my father and his partner were among the fewer than half who reached a mining camp.

"There were all sorts of people among these gold diggers," my father tells Linck. "Some played and soon drank up their profits, but others were wiser and later came back to Seattle with their money. They were interesting days. What a commotion. Seattle began a recovery that has never stopped."

Linck asks him the same question that has dogged my curiosity all along. "Came you over there and you never even wanted to play?"

"Yes, but always gently."

I knew he must have done something besides clear forests, build buildings, read books, and make money. But discretion ruled among the Victorians.

"Found yourself some gold?" Linck continues.

"Not much." My father flicks his fingers. "But I came to know Alaska. And later I obtained a personal interest in a gold mine."

More than one mine. Each of my children have some of their grandfather's defunct stock certificates -- yellowed papers with official seals from the *Alaska Dano Mines Company* and the *Alaska Reindeer Company*.

My father contracted pneumonia after three months on the Yukon River. Believing that he would not survive, his partner abandoned him and left for another camp, later perishing as he returned on the ill-fated steamer, *Clara Nevada,* which sank.

Pederson made it home on another ship. Whether he found a new traveling partner, I don't know. I imagine him with a ratty matted beard and shoes of burlap tied to the top of his boots. Short of food by then, he may have developed scurvy, with bleeding gums and spots peppering his thighs and legs.

But he did make it back to Seattle -- part of a select company who survived a winter in the vast Alaskan wilderness, endured the rushing rapids and exercised their wits while many gave up, or perished.

The experience gave them confidence in what they had overcome as well as respect for what they had not. They attained a level of achievement that later brought many of them into successful leadership positions.

"From then on, a little bit of calm came over me," my father tells Linck.

"Yes, a little bit." Marie interrupts, turning in her chair to smile at her husband.

"Yes it did," he continues. "I now began in earnest to build houses. Sometimes I took on a contract and sometimes I went into partnership with my friend. And then I met my wife after all."

Marie looks down at her hands. I imagine her as being pleasingly plump and patient with her husband. While he developed the business and hired their countrymen, she supported the community resources that enabled care for their families.

"She came by sea with a brother and took a place as a servant girl in a Danish house. There was the wedding, but there was no time for a honeymoon. After the first few years, we took a trip to California. And now ... still to come ... is a trip around the world."

———

But they managed only one more trip to Denmark during the summer of 1931, before Marie died in March of 1932. The Danish-English newspaper *Bien* describes their leave-taking from Seattle's Great Northern depot. Nearly 200 people gathered to see the thirty-one travelers board "The Danish Brotherhood Special," a special train chartered for the occasion.

"The last half hour before leaving Seattle alternated between conversations of business and pleasure with 'King Hans' Pederson. Of course he was wished a good trip by all."

The train then moved on to Spokane to pick up passengers from Southern Washington and Oregon. Other travelers included Mr. Lovgreen – Scandinavian American Line's general agent for Seattle, together with *Bien's* correspondent for the trip, Mr. Albert Odgaard.

I believed Marie to be harsh when I first read of her strict treatment of her niece Laura Madsen, newly arrived in Seattle. Marie sent fifteen-year-old Laura to the butcher with a meat order written in English, but when Laura panicked, the butcher anticipated Marie's order and filled it. Marie understood that Laura would get nowhere until she buckled down and learned English. Her own experience as an immigrant serving in a Danish home had taught Marie that learning English would be essential to Laura's future success in America.

Linck's energy flags long before Pederson's as the visit continues. One day, Linck accompanies him on yet another long ride where he dwells on memories. Pederson takes a letter out of his pocket and murmurs, as he reads it, "Yes, it has been interesting and exciting." He shuts his eyes and forces his mind away as he solves another problem or estimates a job.

"Have you lost money on any large projects?" Linck asks, to bring him back to the present.

He laughs. "Broadmoor farm is actually the only asset that I own outright. A 1907 crash brought a stop to all Seattle cash payments." He describes his losses. He lost money as part owner of the Smith Pier project. He lost $172,000 on a railroad construction project, because during the First World War the workers walked off the job. He lost $125,000 on municipal work for Tacoma. Looking back, he remarks that in those exciting days, profits were secondary. The challenge was in the game, the risk. His current project, the six-story King County Courthouse addition, would keep his men going for a long time in the midst of the 1929 slowdown, of uncertain duration.

"But clever fowl can also handle the nettles." He laughs long and hard as he recalls his accomplishments as a shipbuilder. "The government cancelled a two million dollar contract to build eight ships during World War I, but I was awarded $100,000 for preparatory work."

Linck joins the Pedersons one weekend for a holiday on Fletcher Bay, a cove in Puget Sound. Their host, Dr. Frolund, has a thriving chiropractic practice in natural healing. The group follows the Frolund teenagers through the woods and down the hill to Puget Sound for a swim. Despite the sunshine, the water, only a dozen miles from the Olympic Mountains, is icy cold. Pederson plunges into the water with the young people who soon get out and warm themselves on the beach stones. My father swims on by himself.

During dinner in the shady garden, Dr. Frolund berates conventional medicine. "Humbug! Humbug! It is for the ordinary dead. They are just pulling money out of people's pockets."

Linck decides that Pederson and Dr. Frolund have the same philosophy. Enjoy the brief holiday, but stay ahead of the competition. Work while you can and don't let up.

22. Hearts

My father waves off his philanthropy whenever Linck raises the subject -- the way he'll pay $1,000 for a painting offered for sale at $100; his contributions to hospitals, the YMCA, the Danish Church. A Mason, he built the Scottish Rite Masonic Temple at Broadway and Harvard. He assures Linck it is really his wife who helps people with her small attentions and joys. Marie, a welcome guest at the Danish Old People's Home, can never resist small, orphaned children. "Right now she is supporting an entire family of ten children. They lost their parents," he says.

So one afternoon, he sends Linck over to the Narada to sit with the ailing Mrs. Pederson, a diabetic also plagued with gout, heart, and kidney problems. Linck observes that "the disease has ennobled her face by endowing it with a gentle pull."

"The pain in my legs forces me to lie down. Why should I bother someone when they can't help me?" Marie admits that she groans alone in their rich home. "After a while the pain goes away."

The conversation turns to her husband's restlessness. "He is pouring out his health, filling his head every minute. At night when he can't sleep, he turns on his light and reads. What time do you think he gets up in the morning?" she asks Linck. Not waiting for an answer, she says, "He must be absolutely up at six, take a bath, and be gone before the neighbors."

"Can't you stay here a little longer?" I ask him every morning. "But no. He will not stay in bed when he can't sleep." Hesitantly she tells Linck she has noticed recently that women seem to want to care for him. She wishes he would just bid on work in Seattle. But only that week, a woman persuaded him to go to Portland to bid on building a bridge. And just that morning she learned that he got the job. "In Portland! He is completely impossible," she exclaims with a tired, defeated smile.

But the year was 1929. As banks and businesses failed, my father reached out wherever he could to keep going, to keep his men employed. He was the last major Seattle contractor to hold out while the banks had money to lend.

In their home, Linck notices photos of their son in every room at every age. Marie's voice breaks as she describes the raw pain of losing him those many years ago. "His illness came on so fast that it seemed impossible he might die. He overheard me say that I would be happy to sacrifice my life if I could only save his." She looks down at her hands and rubs one over the other. "Then he said, 'Hush Mama, you must not speak so.'"

Her voice levels as she praises Hans Jr. "Such a good son, so witty and clever, he earned his money himself working so hard for Hans. He had already bought a car." She looks away at the mountains. "On the last day of his life I asked him if his feet were warm. 'Yes, Mama,' he said. But already his feet were cold. You see, he didn't want me to worry."

Her lip trembles as she gazes into the distance. "When he died, Hans stopped working. He adored our son. Hans Jr. was a motherless nephew of mine. You see, Hans never really had a childhood of his own. It was always work for him. And then he left home at an early age to serve in the army. How he reveled in our son's toys and games. How he enjoyed his schooling. But now our hopes lay in ruins. Hans was so bent with grief that he stayed home from work.

"The public display was the worst of all. Strangers. Utter strangers rushed over to us to speak of life and death and religion. Then there was the funeral. The flowers and condolences only made things worse."

Silence fills the gray and drizzling air until Marie admits that the pain of his loss has remained fresh through the years. "We gave away his radio. We couldn't bear to hear it. But we still feel that he is near. We keep the urn with his ashes in his room." She turns to Linck. "Do you think this is selfish? Remember that he was only nineteen years old." She throws up her hands. "We are old and frail now. When I die my ashes will be spread among the forest trees where perhaps they may fertilize the earth for some benefit."

My father speaks also both with resignation and with confidence about Hans Jr. on a later walk in the country with Linck. Slowing his rapid pace, he says, "I consider my son to be my guardian angel. He was so good that he gave everything away. Whenever I am in doubt about what I should do, I think of him." He bends to pick up a twig and snaps it. "I'll tell you a little story. Some time ago I was on a trip to the forest. I planned to make an offer to clear it. Several people with us explored the terrain. I found it to be a wilderness and wandered completely away from the others, so engrossed in some rare berries and flowers that I forgot the time and place.

"I finally realized I was alone. I called out, but no one replied. What to do? I looked everywhere. The road was nowhere in sight." He waves his arm to the right. "'*Go that way,*' said an impulse. I left the designated path and coming to a hill, ascended it. From the top I then saw the road and the wagons of our group. It was my son, my guardian angel, who gave me this inspiration."

He stops in a clearing above a vast forested wilderness. "You might think this a minor thing, you might think maybe, but I felt that it was he. It is he who is with me in each new work. He would not have been my employee for long in life, but in death -- his spirit has been my supervisor." He bends his head and picks up the trail again. "We would be very poor, if we had not raised him."

They continue without speaking as Linck remembers the words of a poet: "*Memory seems as nothing, however, it is the most secret fountain.*"

I grieved with Marie and my father as they remembered their son, my half-brother. It is not difficult to idealize someone you never knew. Using his words, I feel now that my father is my guardian angel - - a guiding voice in sticky times that has enriched my later years. Now I ask myself in troublesome situations, what would he do? I say this, feeling no disloyalty to my adoptive father who raised me with love and high standards. How fortunate I am to have known two fathers instead of none, an outcome that surely creates a void in the life of any child.

———

Olaf Linck closes his visit to the Pedersons with a dinner at their Narada penthouse on Highland Drive. Hans leads him on a tour of the grounds, dashing down the steep five-story stairs where in the early evening Mt. Rainier, sixty miles away, appears wrapped in a dark haze. The eternal snow flames as red gold. Linck tries to keep up with my father as he jumps from ledge to ledge among the terraces of blooming plants at the Victoria Apartments above the Narada where on my first trip to Seattle I had paid a quarter to enjoy the panoramic view.

"The tooth of time will have a hard time gnawing these buildings," my father explains to Linck. "I used burgundy bricks from Montana to get the best stone. Cement is sensitive," he explains. "It reveals different qualities in different climates." He points out the Fionia apartments below them, named after his birthplace, the Isle of Fyn. "Can you see the gardens on top of the roof? I used Danish cement there."

Marie waves to them from the fire escape. They enter the building and take the elevator to the fifth floor to join her for dinner. Among the Royal Copenhagen porcelain that graces the shelves and tables is a charming pair of figurines -- a little girl in a blue dress, her fair hair bobbed with bangs, and a smaller boy in baggy overalls, leaning forward as he takes his first drag on his father's pipe -- the pair that I rescued from the gift shop when my mother tried to sell them.

"But those were my father's," I'd told her, outraged.

"Okay. Take them." She'd shoved them at me to carry home.

The apartment walls are lined with art, much of it purchased at fundraisers. Behind the couch is the central painting: Monsted's snow scene of a woman walking along a shady road in the village of Lillehammer. The oil painting perfectly captures the afternoon shadows in a way that celebrates the peace of winter. My father tells Linck that he bought the painting from the Danish consul when he was recalled to Denmark. Later, on a visit to the U.S., Prince Waldemar told the Pedersons that the king of Denmark owned the only other snow scene by the artist Monsted.

———

I felt guilty when I read this. After Mother died, I found the heavy wooden crate built to contain the painting as it travelled the world. It took three of us to lift it into the U-Haul that we drove to Maine from Greensboro with our share of Mother's things. I hesitated before I sold the massive painting, but the huge snow scene chilled and dominated the north-facing living room of our Maine condo. Until I learned where it had come from, the painting always seemed as pretentious as Mother's pink velvet couch and purple satin drapes. Had I kept it, it would have overpowered any room I have ever lived in. It would have been a constant reminder of my family's deception. Cookie offered to take it. Instead, I sold it.

———

After Marie's dinner of pork chops and potatoes, they sink into comfortable chairs to talk. Linck asks why my father changed the Danish spelling of his given name of Pedersen with an "e" to Pederson, with an "o," because of a misspelling on a stationery order. With his high standards and attention to detail, why did he allow this?

"By then it didn't matter," he said. "Once I built the Ford assembly plant, the Lake Washington Bridge, and the Danish Church, I had no need for a last name. By then, I was known all over Seattle as Hans."

Ford Motor Company 1928, Seattle. Printed with permission: Museum of History & Industry (MOHAI).

When Linck asks if Hans was a bookworm in school, Mrs. Pederson sets down her needlework and says, "He sat at the top."

Growing more expansive, my father loses his customary modesty. "Yes, I was number one, and I was indeed at the top in church when I was confirmed. I reached the top in most trades, for example, in arithmetic calculation as well as Denmark's history and geography. I was also the strongest boy in school and could comfortably pass the others when we wrestled."

The Pedersons' bookcase is filled with books that show the ties to their homeland: a Danish history of Icelandic sagas, Jacob Knudsen, whose novels explore the conflict between society and conscience, Holberg's comedies as well as Henrik Ibsen. English works include Darwin, Shakespeare, Spencer as well as books about Napoleon, the French Revolution, and American history.

Mrs. Pederson again sets down her needlework and says, "My husband has often recited large sections of Shakespeare's plays and poems that he remembers by heart."

"Have you written poems?" Linck asks.

"Who hasn't? But only for my own pleasure."

Pederson describes his return to Denmark in 1917 and his disappointment when his old teacher couldn't remember him. "I returned to the manor oak forest that had cast such a spell on me as a child. In the manor garden, I had imagined that I was in Crete playing Theseus. I found my way through the labyrinth by the Princess Ariadne's guiding line. Now it was so easy to find my way out of it." A faraway look comes into his eyes. "Yet, it was nice to come home and see the old places again. I felt homesick for Denmark."

Still, Linck believes that Hans Pederson remains a modest man. His quotations demonstrate his learning.

"A man must renounce something by winning in business," my father says. "I have lost spiritual respect. What I have acquired from windows and doors and bricks, I cannot take with me."

His wife nods as if to say, "That's what I have always said. What are all the buildings for?"

He shakes his silvered head. "I would not have it another way. I learned through experience to estimate what a work should cost. It has been my strength that I understand all kinds of buildings. I understand engineering as well as bricklaying. I can monitor the Broadmoor farm, as well as my grandparents' house in the village of Stenstrup. I keep track of the finest details. This is why I have been busier than other builders."

The men move to the balcony where they look down over the illuminated city that fifty years earlier had been a forest. Pederson's Fox Theater flashes commercials. The lights change constantly. Not a sound reaches them from the festive city below. Who would have dreamed that Hans Pederson would become so famous in the Pacific Northwest where the boats spin like luminous beetles.

23. My Parents

Olaf Linck sailed back to Denmark to write his biography of Hans Pederson, published a year later, 1930, in Denmark. Construction slowed as the Depression spread its ruinous tentacles ever farther. No major building would rise in downtown Seattle for twenty years. My father, now sixty-six years old, had four apartment buildings nearing completion -- the Bering, the Viking, the Westroy, and the Iris.

In their 1970s articles, Hyde and White note that when most building projects fell apart in 1930, Pederson held out the longest. Both of them reported on a version of Pederson's conversation with the three bank executives who refused to loan him any more money. White's version follows:

"I started these buildings with the understanding that you would advance the money to finish them."

"We could not see then what was going to happen. No money is being advanced to any builder."

"You men know me. You have never changed your minds before when a building was not finished. The Bering is all ready except installation of the elevator, the laying of hall carpets, and some painting."

"We are sorry, Mr. Pederson. We simply cannot advance any money."

"Nothing can be rented in the buildings the vay they are," Pederson said, with his typical Danish inflection.

"We know that."

"You vant to get back the money you already loaned me?"

"Of course. We know you will pay us."

"You ever been in the apartment house business?" Pederson asked them with a slow smile. He knew these bankers better than they thought he did.

"No, we have never been in the business."

Pederson rose and turned to go. Back over his shoulder he said, "I pay all I owe you right now -- with four unfinished apartment buildings." He glanced at the clock. It was ten minutes to twelve. "From noon your bank is in business. In case you should vant a good contractor to finish some buildings, I vill bid on the job, but my bid vill have to be higher than the amount I vant to borrow."

By twelve o'clock the bankers were smiling, and Pederson had his money exactly as had been originally promised. The Bering, the Viking, the Westroy and the Iris were speedily finished."

His triumph was short lived. Business came to a standstill. Rather than despair, my father developed other interests. Elected a director of the Seattle Baseball Club in 1931, he also took his ailing wife Marie and thirty one Seattle Danes on one last "Danish Brotherhood Special" visit to the old country.

In March, two months before they left, Marie drew a new will leaving all her property to Hans and naming him as executor. In the event that he predeceased her, she listed ten pages of bequests totaling $250,000 -- $10,000 to her niece, Millie Dines, and the same amount to two of her Madsen nephews. In addition, she left between $1,000-$6,000 to twenty-two relatives, $1,000 to eighteen friends, and also eleven $5,000 trusts to the children of relatives. She did not forget her favorite charities -- The Northwest Danish Old People's Home and the Children's Orthopedic Hospital of Seattle. Any residue would go to the Danish Children's Home of Tyler, Minnesota. Should Hans die, or be unable to serve as executor, Marie directed Hans' bookkeeper, Stahl, along with her two nephews, to administer the will that would keep the money under their control.

Hans did not witness his wife's will. The years had also taken their toll on his health. Plagued with six years of increasing hypertension that began in 1925, he suffered a stroke late in 1931 after they returned from their trip to Denmark. Back then, my doctor told me, there were no medications for hypertension. You just waited for the stroke. Conventional wisdom indicated that blood pressure naturally rose with age. A reading of 230/130 might be expected with the elderly.

The trip to Denmark left Marie in a weakened state. Not much could be done for her. A diabetic for eleven years before the use of insulin, she had gone through a series of caregivers, beginning with her niece, Laura Madsen. Now her kidneys were shutting down and her heart was failing as well.

With construction at an end, Marie's life on a downward course, and his own declining health, Hans could no longer escape to his office with its sign on the wall, GET YOUR HAPPINESS OUT OF YOUR WORK OR YOU WILL NEVER KNOW WHAT HAPPINESS IS. Little happiness remained in his life. Not only were his wife and his business empire failing, he was also forced to terminate his loyal employees. The banks wouldn't lend him money. His tenants couldn't pay the rent. What did he care anymore for money? His goal had always been to create buildings of use and beauty — to provide a living for his men. Now, with no heir, his immediate family consisted of two half-sisters and a half-brother in Denmark. If he died before Marie, her relatives would inherit his assets.

Of course, he and Marie had been a part of the Danish community for forty years. He had built Washington Hall for the Danish Brotherhood in 1908 to house the needs of the growing Seattle Danish population. According to the Washington State Department of Archaeology, the building served for sixty-five years as a boardinghouse for Seattle's newly-arrived Danish immigrants, and also as a social gathering place. The Danish Brotherhood and Sisterhood met in the Lodge Room on different weekdays. Washington Hall continues to anchor the Squire Park neighborhood as a social and musical performance hall. The Historic Seattle organization raised $15,000,000 and renovated the building in 2016.

Hans must have sunk into a personal depression, knowing that on the Seattle waterfront below his Queen Anne Hill penthouse, the

Skid Row and Hooverville slums grew steadily -- hovels pieced together from packing crates and scrap lumber.

The last time Victor White went to my father's office, he found him hunched over his roll-top desk, arms folded, with only the back of his head showing under his thatch of thick white hair. His shoulders heaving, he wept because the bank had cut off his cash. He wanted to build more apartments so he could keep his men working. Most were Scandinavians with families, men who had spent their entire working lives with him. So after Pederson's contracting business died, he moved into the rental business -- hiring managers to collect the rents, pay the mortgages, and maintain the buildings. When his tenants stopped paying their rent, he absorbed most of the losses himself. Soon he owed interest on tax delinquencies.

The Omaha, Nebraska newspaper, *Den Danske Pioneer*, noted Marie's death in March of 1932.

"[Tr.] Mrs. Hans Pedersen is dead. This Sunday came as a wildfire the sad tidings that Mrs. Hans Pederson, 25 W. Highland Drive, suddenly had passed away. A faithful wife, who for the last 6 months with loving care nursed her sick husband, has now even herself bowed to death. Mrs. Pederson was very much loved by everyone who came in contact with her. Especially the sick and most severely tried persons, she had passion in their trouble, and she was always willing to help a good cause.

She was buried the 9th March. It was one of the major funerals among the Danes here for a long time. The chapel was filled with flowers and many friends showed their sympathy."

Marie's death certificate notes that her niece, Millie Dines, not Hans, reported Marie's death to the authorities. Perhaps Millie had been caring for the Pedersons at their penthouse. Millie and her Madsen cousins, essentially the Pedersons' Seattle family, must have provided much support and concern for their Aunt Marie and Uncle Hans as their medical problems increased along with their ages. Each of them stood to inherit $10,000 if Aunt Marie survived Uncle Hans. But since she hadn't, their inheritances were no longer assured.

Even though Marie's will named Hans as executor, he left the project to her alternate executors; Stahl, his trusted business manager, and Marie's nephews. On the day of Marie's 1932 death, Stahl conducted an immediate inventory of the Pederson assets: real estate, bank accounts, receivables, investments, personal property, mortgages, contracts, leases, insurance and accounts payable. Back in 1920, Hans had added Marie as an owner to some of his business interests. When my friend Don obtained the death certificates and wills for Marie and Hans at the King County Courthouse, he noted more than eighty pages of claims against Hans' estate; enough to take up part of a microfiche tape. But Marie's affairs filled three entire microfiche tapes.

"It was hard to tell who owned what," Don said.

The inventory of assets before the deducting of any liabilities was $1,315,318. My mother's 200 pages of legal documents reveal the conflict and complexity that kept the Pedersons' assets in limbo for nine years. No wonder Hans was known as a king. No wonder Marie's relatives felt that $250,000 was a reasonable share of assets to claim. Tensions mounted as time went on. During the nine-year settlement process, a judge ordered Marie's executors to curtail their excessive withdrawals. Millie Dines, who was not an executor, sued to obtain her $10,000 share. Mom and Dad thought she should get nothing.

What the documents do not reveal are the contents of the 32 pages that were removed from Mother's records. I expect those pages contained material that Mother did not want anyone to see. Names of people who contested the estate, who made life so unpleasant for her that she chose to marry Everett, the man she met on a cruise, the man who would get her out of Seattle into a fascinating life of luxurious world travel.

The lure of money brings surprises. Those closest to Hans Pederson felt a sense of entitlement that brought out their fighting spirits when they learned that they would have to compete for a succession of dwindling funds, most of which had evaporated in debt. Marie's nieces and nephews sued. In one of Dad's China letters to Mother, he wrote that it would become her if she should turn out to be a millionairess. Instead, the estate's final meager tally embittered her.

Hans and Marie chose to use their assets to benefit the community. During a time of economic privation, their estates also provided a lifeline to their lawyers, accountants, managers, and creditors in Seattle; the city where the Pedersons had built their lives. Bookkeeper Stahl's 233 pages of detailed accounting records were filled with entries large and small -- including three separate payments to the newly created Social Security System for $.50, $1.68, and $1.75.

But soon, the man who had wept for his son, wept for his wife, and wept for his men, wept no more. Shortly after his trip to Denmark in 1931, he had fallen out of a tree while picking cherries, suffered a rupture, and subsequently, a stroke. He had recuperated with mineral baths and rubdowns at a sanitarium at Soap Lake, so named because the foam formed by its minerals resemble soapsuds. Indian artifacts point to Soap Lake's long use as a place of healing by Indian tribes. In Pederson's day it was frequented as a health spa. Victor White, who knew my father in the prime of his life, stated that my mother nursed him back to health at Soap Lake.

Shortly before she died, Mother told me she had met my father in the elevator of the Narada where she was on her way to visit someone else in this expensive apartment residence. Possibly Hans, remembering her from Soap Lake, hired her to be his nurse after Marie died. Millie Dines may have hired her since Millie reported both Marie and Hans' deaths to the authorities. Whoever informed the newspapers of Hans' death noted only my name, not my mother's on both obituaries.

Since there were no medications for hypertension, by that time Hans may have also been suffering from mini-strokes and episodic heart ailments. No doubt his lifetime diet of steak, pork, eggs, and cheese contributed to narrowed arteries. Millie Dines may have also moved into the Narada, not only to help with nursing duties, but also to keep an eye on Hans, smitten with the comely nurse. One reason for Marie's hastily-drawn will may have been that her family, as well as Marie, had observed the attentions of younger women to Hans, sometimes called "the youngest man in Seattle."

Mom was always evasive about her time as a nurse. "Oh, for a little while," she'd say, and move on. That short time of nursing care must have been the part of my mother's Seattle experience that landed her in the right place at the right time in order to "do what I had to," as she told her Hushlak niece, Mary Ann. Both Mother's sisters, Helen and Alice, told me that Mom was my father's nurse.

Ever a man of vision, Hans brushed aside advancing years and declining health to woo his beautiful twenty-five-year old nurse, Dorris (as he misspelled it) — the woman who would become my mother. There they were in the Narada, tripping over each other all day. Marie had told Olaf Linck that women called Hans with projects. They wanted to care for him. Now he had found one that he could care for. She too had grown up on a farm. Not much older than the son he had lost five years earlier, she was smart and courageous — a pioneer woman and a raving beauty to boot.

For whatever time he had left, he would live. There was no denial of impending death; sooner or later there would be another stroke or a heart attack. He had weakened. He set to wooing Dorris, encouraging her to tell him about her difficult childhood. He too had left behind a life of bare subsistence. He praised her courage, her drive, her intelligence -- her mastery of English, a second language for both of them. Seeking opportunity, both of them had risked their futures by joining the hordes of immigrants to America. Dorris, like Marie, had backbone. Here was Hans' chance to leave more than a legacy of buildings. Here was his chance to produce an heir with the lovely Dorris.

His pursuit must have been relentless. He knew how to get what he wanted. All that drive, all that testosterone had made him the envy of his colleagues. How much time did he have left to explore Dorris' perfect body, to feast his eyes on her flawless face, her nose with its upward-tilt that matched the lilt in her melodious Canadian voice. How much time did he have left to produce an heir?

Dorris acquiesced. She agreed to marry her elderly patient, forty-two years her senior. On the waterfront below Pederson's double Narada penthouse, its walls lined with art, festered the crazy-quilt shanties of Skid Row and Hooverville. The desperate life that might be her alternative became unthinkable. Hans was old, but he was rich, successful, and kind — one of Seattle's most respected leaders, a man known throughout the city by his first name. There was no question that he was failing. His hands shook. He could barely sign his name. She'd seen his blood pressure shoot to the stratosphere. Hans had mangy hair and dark circles under his eyes. She knew what the ravages of hypertension would soon bring. But he was still on his feet. She probably reasoned that after a short marriage, his wealth would envelop and protect her for the rest of her life.

Of course, he might demand his marital rights. Did he have the vigor? Probably not. She knew his careless personal habits, the way he nodded off after meals. Recalling the old men in her life, I imagine she pushed the thought to the back of her mind. She may have remembered the family story about Grandfather Tokaruk tending his crops by the side of the road wearing only his dingy union suit, telling the red-coated Mounties to get out; he'd wear whatever he wanted on his own land. Or perhaps she thought of her drunken father Wasyl. Sure he'd played the violin, but she pushed away the memories of the times she'd hidden from him, the times he'd made a fool of himself on his way home from the tavern. None of her family could hold their heads up in the town of Andrew.

When she thought about it, Hans might be almost like the father she had always wanted.

In his *Frontier Times* article, Victor White describes the way Hans Pederson amazed everybody with his next move. His bookkeeper Stahl told White that Pederson walked into his office in the Washington Mutual Savings Building one morning and headed straight for the safe. He kneeled, spun the dial, and removed a sheaf of papers. Stahl watched and wondered, knowing the safe contained no cash. The papers were life insurance policies that Pederson had carried for years, policies that named the banks as beneficiaries should anything happen to him in the midst of a project. The banks had loaned him money on his word — his word was his bond. Pederson knew he would never build again, so those policies were his with no further obligation.

"What're you going to do with them, Hans?" Stahl asked.

He grinned like a happy kid. "I'm going to cash them in and go on a honeymoon."

Stahl told White he just stood there gaping while Pederson stuffed the policies in his pocket. At the door, he said, "You fellows can vind things up better than I can anyvay. There's nothing more to build, and I vouldn't touch any money in the business till things get straightened out."

What he did was totally in character. His honesty would not let him draw money from a business with uncertain assets and numerous liabilities. As for Mother, awed by his success and his lifestyle, I doubt that she understood she was marrying a gambler who had always thrived on risk.

In August 1932, five months after Marie's death, the Danish American newspaper Bien reported, "Builder Hans Pederson and his young wife left Seattle with the purpose of visiting Olympia in Southern California."

A small announcement in the Seattle newspaper's business, not society section, announced my parents' marriage. Never one to seek publicity, my father knew enough to protect his young bride from the slings and arrows that would come their way with the accusation that she had married him for his money. She must have been grateful for her newfound security. She may have felt like a guest living in the home he had shared with Marie. Soon pregnant with me, I doubt that she had much interest in redecorating or altering another woman's furnishings. She knew her life with Hans would be brief. One of the first things she did after their honeymoon was to bring her sisters, Helen and Alice, to visit from Canada. Many years later, both of them told me how nice Hans was. Helen was impressed with their double penthouse filled with art. Alice said, "He seemed old. But when you're nineteen, most adults seem old."

My father needed a reason to live. He needed a nurse to care for him. My mother needed a home and security. I hope they were happy in their penthouse overlooking Elliott Bay and the Olympic Mountains, Mother doing what she had to, yet living in more luxury than she had ever imagined with a sick old man whose strength was his character.

White closes his article, "Hans Pederson's accomplishments received so little publicity that I doubt if there are a dozen people who know as much about his career as I have related here, or if all the newspaper clippings and library books would reveal as much."

I am speculating about the early life and motives of my parents. I come not to snoop, but to understand. I try to imagine their brief life together, shutting out the world. I hope their short marriage brought them what they needed at the time. I hope that my father felt his youth and vitality restored before his final stroke, and that my mother felt protected and loved. Back then she probably spent two weeks in the hospital when I was born. My father must have had the stroke shortly after she came home. They must have succeeded in maintaining their privacy, since my father's obituaries in both the *Seattle Daily Times* and the *Seattle Post Intelligencer* mention my name, but not Mother's.

I wonder how the reporters got this information. Was my father was well enough to call the newspapers to announce my birth? Had he called, wouldn't they have reported my Mother's name? Perhaps they spoke to Marie's family who chose to announce only the name of Hans' heir. That also seems unlikely given their shock at Hans marrying such a young woman within months of Marie's death. Imagine their reaction.

Something is missing here. I sometimes wonder what Mercer, our Philadelphia attorney, learned when Mr. Moriarty spoke to his mother in 1984. When Mercer told me, "You may be the best thing that ever happened to her," (my mother), I was too shaken to ask anything else. I don't really know why Mom carefully tore 32 pages out of my father's 233-page estate settlement.

My mother, who hid her nursing background, never hesitated to display her business acumen. My parents married in July 1932. They conceived me that November. Four months later, Hans drew a new will, revoking all previous wills for two stated reasons: *"First, the present economic condition has greatly reduced the value of my estate; second, I expect to soon become a father and I strongly feel that I should amply provide for my wife Dorris Ann Pederson and our expected child."*

He named Mother as executor without bond. Unlike Marie's executors, each of them bonded for $5,000, Mom could spend whatever she wanted to settle his estate. His intentions were clear. He construed his will as a non-intervention will, without notice or confirmation of any court. One witness, his physician, had also attended Marie during her illnesses. Although my father's shaky signature on his will indicated his weak physical condition, his doctor attested that he was of sound mind.

I hope that he was well enough to enjoy my first days on this earth. Mother told me that both Hans and her own father died when cars struck them. The similarity makes me further question her memory of her father. She seemed to resent that Hans Pederson abandoned her by dying before he collected what was owed him. She was left with a newborn and a legal mess. I have to wonder if she resented me too. It seems as if her revenge was to keep him a secret from me. Perhaps my father Hans brought back frightening childhood memories of her own father. Did she see them both as molesters who instead should have been protectors?

She never found lasting security from any of the men in her life. One day, as we spoke of Dad, my stepfather, she said, "I married him to take care of me, but now I have to take care of him."

After my birth she felt the sense of abandonment, or perhaps betrayal, that plagued her the rest of her life. Her parents had little time to care for her. Ever loyal to her younger siblings, she had often been their childhood caretaker. She put up with her old husband, because he fulfilled her longing for security. He rescued her from an uncertain future, but now he was dying, leaving her with a tiny baby. She deserved better.

How frantic she must have been as Hans Pederson lay at home in the bed where he died, his skin swollen from failing kidneys, his fingers pale and groping. As she tried to meet the simultaneous demands of her dying husband and her newborn daughter, far from the support of her own large family, she must have felt overwhelmed and alone.

Mother had a living will. I have a living will. Hans lived at a time before living wills were necessary to prevent needless prolonging of death with myriad machines. Hopelessly ill, he was bedridden under her care. His doctor listed his cause of death as a cerebral hemorrhage.

Sixteen months later, in January 1935, Mother petitioned for U.S. citizenship by amending the Declaration of Intent she had filed in 1929 under yet another name, Domnica Hutsuliak. Her request for citizenship as Doris Pederson also included me — Paula Tynia Pederson, a middle name she never once mentioned to me.

Later in January she married Everett, left Seattle forever and closeted my father's memory. Mother never wanted it known that she had been his nurse. Escape eluded her as shame or bad memories tormented her the rest of her life. She kept neither a photo of my father, nor a copy of his biography.

Mother chose to remember Hans by his valuables. She kept the huge Monsted painting, the Royal Copenhagen figurines, the silverware, and the worthless stock certificates. She gave her engagement ring to my eldest son, Jeff, but never showed it to me.

I expect a numerologist might find meaning in the round numbers that mark the dates of my parents' deaths.

Hans Pederson   09/06/1933

Domka Huculak   09/06/1999

His end was our beginning.

Acknowledgements

This story would still be in my head had it not been for the help of so many others. First of all, my editor and publisher, Wendy Wiley of Seattle's VIE Communication. VIE's staff and Robert Wiley, met the challenge of authenticating Hans Pederson's contracting work with much historical research that I never could have pursued from the east coast. Wendy is a versatile wonder. Her mark matches her creative artistry and publishing acumen.

Everything I know about Denmark I have learned through blogging where I met Danish blogger mariaholm51 and her husband Henry Jorgensen. Genealogist Henry unearthed 80-year old news articles about Hans Pederson, and then sent me translations. They took me on a photographic tour through Stenstrup on the Isle of Fyn, the Danish village where my father spent his childhood.

Charlene and Don Vollmer made their home a hospitable haven whenever I came to Seattle. They spent untold hours reading this work. They travelled all over the city, sending me updates on their research. Susan Haris and Otto Brask helped me learn about my father's life as one of Seattle's early Scandinavian settlers. David Schlosser and the Pacific Northwest Writers Association (PNWA) kept me posted on Seattle's vibrant writing life.

Bob Cushman kindly offered editing tips along with his careful proofreading eye. He, Judy Day and Larry Miller offered me their homes as writing studios when they were away. A quiet place to concentrate is every writer's dream! Early on, Debra Leigh Scott's Hidden River Arts Foundation awarded me a retreat where I could explore my material.

Davidson College professor Shireen Campbell taught me about memoir writing. She encouraged me to believe that I could write this book. She helped shape the story and edited the manuscript. Charlotte, NC author Judy Goldman told me, "this is the book you must write."

My loving thanks to Mike and my children for their patience through the years. Grateful praise is due to the following readers for their suggestions as the tale evolved. Margaret Bigger, Sue and Harvey Gerry, Priscilla and Bill Ambrose, Meredith and Myron Hamer, Ellie and Walter Christie, Joan Grander and Gordon West, and Gail Powell.

Hans Pederson's Construction

Partial list

Note: As a Dane, his name should have been spelled Pedersen, but a stationery order delivered to him misspelled his name as Pederson, so he kept this spelling since another Seattle contractor spelled his name Pedersen.

Pederson and his family or his construction company had a part in the building or development of the following list of buildings in the Puget Sound area.

Seattle Buildings

Arctic Club - 3rd Ave. at Cherry St.
Alaska Bldg. - plastered first all steel
  skyscraper
Bremer Grocery
King County Courthouse addition
  (6 stories) former County/City building,
  516 Third Ave.
Henry Ford Assembly Plant
Masonic Temple - 1608 4th Ave. W
NW Danish Old People's Home
Northwest Hospital - 1550 N 115th St
Prefontaine - 400 Yesler Way
Sam Hunter - 2911 First Ave.
Seaboard - 1500 4th Ave.
Oregon Timber
Terminal Sales - 1923 1st Ave.
Washington Hall - 153 14th Ave.

Hotels

Liberty Court
Milwaukee
New Washington
Northern Snohomish (old wooden)
Spring Apartment
St. Regis

Theaters

Alhambra Mayflower
  (was Fox, renamed Wilkes)
Blue Mouse Theatre
Baker
Jackson St.
McGovern's Music Hall
Pantages Theatre
  NE corner Univ. St. & 3rd Ave.
  (renamed Palomar 1936,
  torn down 1964)

Apartments

Pederson built or owned 39 apartment buildings a few are listed below

Bremer
Del Roy
El Capitain
Fionia
Iris
Narada Apartments,
  25 Highland Dr.
Northgate
Spring
Victoria
Viking
Westport

Schools

William Cullen Bryant
Alexander Hamilton
James Madison
Chinese Benevolent Association

Other

Elliott Bay Piers
  15th Ave. NW bridge & viaduct
Smith's Cove dock & pier
Spokane Street viaduct
Locks at Longview

Elsewhere

Bridge, Edmonds
County Roads and Bridges
Medical Dental Bldg., Klamath Falls
National Realty Bldg., Tacoma
Nisqually Power Plant, Tacoma (Tacoma Electric Works, Lost $70,000)
Northern Pacific Tunnels (work when he first arrived)
Portland Municipal Auditorium
Puget Sound bank Bldg., 1920 Tacoma (tallest skyscraper on the coast) Road
building and reclamation projects throughout Washington Temple of Justice,
Olympia Dam across the Yakima River and other parts of the Kittitas
Reclamation Project

Family Archive Photos

Editor's Note:

You may view a collection of family photos from the early
to mid 1900s including many contributed by Tracy Dines
Howes, granddaughter of Millie Madsen Dines.

Hans and Marie were guardians of Millie and her two
brothers. Please visit online at: PaulaPederson.com or on
Facebook at: https://www.facebook.com/MysteriousBuilder/

About the Author

Paula Pederson started her life journey in Seattle, Washington, but has lived in Singapore, Shanghai, Honolulu, New York, New Jersey, Maine and North Carolina. Educated abroad and on the east coast, Pederson's elite schooling taught her much about the nuances of social echelons and how that affects one's life choices.

Her greatest challenge and reward has come from being the mother of five and grandmother of five. Parenting enlightened her insight into her own complicated relationship with her mother and fueled her desire to find out about her father Hans Pederson.

Armed with this accumulated life experience and consumed with curiosity, Pederson's quest to find her father in spite of her mother's reticence became a passion later in life.

Her fiction and nonfiction writing includes two unpublished novels, this memoir and a weekly blog. She formerly enjoyed technical writing and editing posts pertaining to medical, environmental, and engineering issues. Earlier years included development work for schools and handicapped children. She graduated from Smith College with a degree in English Literature and spent one glorious summer as a seaside gardener in a resort on the coast of Maine.

Pederson writes about immigrants and pioneers who came by train to Northwestern North America, expatriates to the Far East, and her love for Maine. She believes fragments of the past help us to understand who we are. Hunting for her father's legacy and writing *The Mysterious Builder Of Seattle Landmarks: The Search for My Father*, has shown her the timeless imprint family leaves on husbands, wives, daughters, sons, and grandchildren.

Bibliography

Books

Alberta Community Development. *Ukrainian Cultural Heritage Village Guide.* Edmonton: Alberta Community Development Historic Sites Service, 1995.

Bagley, Clarence B. *History of Seattle from the Earliest Settlement to the Present Time.* 3 vols. Chicago: Pioneer, 1916.

Berton, Pierre. *The Klondike Fever: The Life and Death of the Last Great Gold Rush.* New York: Alfred A. Knopf, Inc. 1958.

Crowley, Walt. *Historic Photos of Seattle.* Nashville: Turner Publishing Co., 2006.

Hanford, C.H., Ed. *Seattle and Environs, 1852-1924.* Chicago: Pioneer, 1924.

Huchulak, Genevieve, and Shulko, Judy. *Nashee [tr. Ours, a Family History].* Self-published, 2011.

James, Diana E. *Shared Walls: Seattle Apartment Buildings, 1900-1939.* Jefferson, NC and London: McFarland and Company, 2011.

Linck, Olaf. *Danskere Under Stjernebanneret - Emigrant Skaebner i de Forenedi Stater. Bygnestur i Seattle.* Chapter in [tr. *The Danes Under the Stars and Stripes - The Fate of Some Emigrants in the United States of America.]* Copenhagen, Kristiania, 1922.

Linck, Olaf. *Kong Hans ved Stillehavet, Eventyret om den fynske Husmandsson, der er blevet den store Bygmester i Seattle.* [tr. *The Story of a Smallholder's Son From Fyn Who Became Seattle's Great Architect.]* Copenhagen: NYT Nordisk Forlag – Arnold Busck, 1930.

Lukoff, Benjamin. *Seattle Then and Now.* San Diego: Thunder Bay Press, 2010.

Morgan, Murray. *Skid Road: An Informal Portrait of Seattle, rev. ed.* New York: Viking Press, Inc. 1951. Seattle: University of Washington Press Paperback Edition, 1982.

Ochsner Jeffrey Karl and Anderson, Dennis Alan. *Distant Corner: Seattle Architects and the Legacy of H.H. Richardson.* Seattle: Univ. of WA Press, 2003.

Pierce, J. Kingston. *Eccentric Seattle.* Pullman: Washington State University Press, 2003.

Rasmussen, Janet E. *New Land New Lives, Scandinavian Immigrants to the Pacific Northwest.* Northfield: Norwegian-American Historical Assn. Seattle: University of Washington Press, 1993.

Smith, Celeste Louise and Pheasant-Albright, Julie D. *Private Clubs of Seattle.* Charleston: Arcadia Publishing, 2009.

Warburton, Anne. *Signposts to Denmark.* Copenhagen, Hernov Publishers, 1992.

Williams, David B. *Too High & Too Steep: Reshaping Seattle's Topography.* Seattle, University of Washington Press, 2015.

Wilson, William H. *Shaper of Seattle: Reginald Heber Thomson's Pacific Northwest.* Pullman: Washington State University Press, 2009.

Periodicals and Newspapers

Balch, Albert S. "Hans Pederson, A Master Builder," *Seattle Municipal News.*, September 28, 1929.

The Christian Science Monitor. "Any Job to Keep his Men at Work, Pederson Motto," March 27, 1931.

Bien Danish American Newspaper, Hans and Marie Pederson Notices. 29 May, 1931; 10 March 1932; August 4, 1932.

Den Danske Pioneer, Hans and Marie Pederson Notices. Omaha, NE: 27 Aug., 1931; 17 March 1932; 14 September 1933.

Duravetz, George. "Ukranian Immigration to Canada 1891-1914" The Ukranian Canadian Magazine, Kobzar Publishing, Sept. 1988, 24-29. Taras Shevchenko Museum, Toronto, Ontario, Canada

Historic Seattle Preservation Foundation. "*Preservation News: Washington Hall.*" Volume 41//, Issue 2, September 2015.

Hyde, Clinton M. "Forgotten Contractor Left Imprint -- in Sidewalks," *Seattle Times Sunday Magazine,* August 27, 1978, p. 6-7.

Johnson Kirk. "In Seattle, A Sinking Feeling About a Troubled Tunnel." *New York Times,* December 14, 2014.

"Seattle Arctic Club Hotel." *New York Times,* October 31, 2008

Seattle Post Intelligencer. "Hans Pederson, Contractor, Dies: Name Lives On," Sept 7, 1933.

Seattle Times. "Hans Pederson, Long Seattle Resident, Dies," Sept. 7, 1933.

The Christian Science Monitor. "Any Job to Keep His Men at Work, Pederson Motto." March 27, 1931.

White, Victor H. "Seattle's Little Known Dynamo," *Frontier Times,* June July 1973, pp. 18-21 and 56-60.

Electronic Media

Canada: A Country by Consent: "Alberta & Saskatchewan Created: *Laurier's Government Welcomes Immigrants 1900s.*
http://www.canadahistoryproject.ca/ 1905-07-immigrants.html

Chelsey, Frank. "Goon Dip (ca 1862-1933." HistoryLink.org, Essay 9036, May 26, 2009.

Curtis, Edward S. "Princess Angeline, Daughter of Chief Seattle." Historylinkelementary.org, Essay 10737, March 2, 2014

de Coster, Dotty. "Arctic Building (Seattle)." HistoryLink.org, Essay 9462, October 21, 2010.

Encyclopedia of Washington State History. *The Arctic Club.*

Washington State Department of Archaeology and Historic Preservation. *Seattle_- Washington_Hall_01.* By wadahp | Published October 25, 2010

"Klondike Gold Rush." Wikipedia. En.wikipedia.org/*wiki/Seattle_Public_Library.*

"LaGrande Dam." *Tacoma Public Utilities.* http://mytpu.org/tacomapower/about-tacoma-power /dams-power-sources/hydrp-power/nisqually-river-project/

Epilogue

Writing this book has made me a new person. Delving into my family history and studying the lives of my three parents has brought me from judgmental intolerance to a place of compassionate understanding.

Now I ask, "what lies beneath the surface?" whenever I meet someone or visit a new place. It took me years to learn what was behind my mother's sudden rages, her fear of discovery. On several visits to Seattle I traipsed unthinkingly up and down the city's hills before I learned why the land rises and sinks as it does.

I left Seattle when I was two, spent my early childhood abroad, and have lived ever since on the east coast. Once I began to study Hans Pederson's life, and grasped the influence of Seattle's topography and history upon his work, I realized that the scope of the story was beyond the few sources I had found. As my research continued into this city of out-sized ideas and superlatives, I discovered my father's name connected with so many buildings, roads, sidewalks, bridges, and water projects, that it seemed he might have singlehandedly built the northwest.

How could I find expert help on the ground in Seattle? Chance played a part two years later when one evening, my gregarious husband found Wendy Wiley at a Seattle dinner party.

321

As I mingled with the guests in the living room, he ambled into the kitchen and observed the chef preparing a succulent salmon fillet. "And what do you do?" he asked her. "I publish books," she said and we were off. Wendy has sailed through myriad and ever-changing development tasks. She has created an incisive title, artistic cover, clarifying edits, and built technical layouts. Simultaneously Robert Wiley has followed the trail of Pederson's construction. His detective work and title searches have established my father as the managing contractor of several Seattle landmarks. Robert has placed Hans' work squarely in the first third of 20th century Seattle.

I learned that the smattering of what I knew about the early days of the northwest equaled my murky understanding about my parents' lives. It took several years of excavating— digging in, scooping out, and filling in before I could build this book.

I'm the daughter of a prospector from the Klondike Gold Rush of 1898 and here I am sending out a weekly Word Press blog with links to Facebook and LinkedIn. The Internet and social media have brought me full bore into the 21st century.

I started this memoir wondering how to organize the story. I soon learned that unless you are a household name, writing today is of necessity a multimedia experience. Blogging has helped me make friends all over the world. Blogging has brought me a new Danish family. Maria Holm and Henry Jorgensen have guided me through their country's history and culture. They invited me to join them on a photographic tour of my father's birthplace in Stenstrup on the Isle of Fyn, a Danish village that retains its old-fashioned charm. Henry, a genealogist, discovered and translated information about my parents that exists nowhere else.

Lies and secrets hurt families. I've met new cousins and learned hidden truths. The biography that I planned to write about Hans Pederson has turned instead into an understanding of the lives of my three parents as well as my own coming of age story.

This book demonstrates the continuing influence of family through the years — of kinship both genetic and adoptive. This book has brightened my life.

As we bloggers say when someone new checks out our website --

Thanks for stopping by.
Paula
PaulaPederson.com

Index

CPSIA information can be obtained
at www.ICGtesting.com
Printed in the USA
BVHW041321260719
554455BV00012B/77/P